LOVING OURSELVES

LOVING OURSELVES

RAY ASHFORD

FORTRESS PRESS   Philadelphia

Library of Congress Catalog Card Number 76-62604
ISBN 0-8006-1255-8

6193I76   Printed in U.S.A.   1-1255

To the memory
of my parents

CONTENTS

1.

THE ALL-IMPORTANCE OF LOVING OURSELVES

One afternoon I was with a small group of people when the conversation got around to the subject of self-love. It was not a particularly serious discussion until one of the members of our group, a young woman who had not spoken much up to that point, said flatly, "I hate myself." Her jolting statement was followed by an awkward silence.

A little taken aback by the girl's self-disclosure and, I must admit, anxious to see the conversation get back into more conventional channels, I suggested, "You're kidding. You're not serious."

"I couldn't be more serious," she replied. "I've hated myself, really hated myself, for a long time."

As I looked at her, I thought of the gray, quiet hell in which she had been living for several years, and I realized that what she had told us was profoundly true.

Fortunately there are not many of us who, like that young woman, loathe and despise ourselves. We may not, of course, have the utmost in self-esteem, but usually we manage at least to tolerate ourselves. Much less comfortable, though, are the multitudes of people who have a dismally low opinion of themselves and who therefore punish and reject themselves.

1

Some years ago, in a manic eruption of rage, a young doctor murdered his only child. Committed to an institution for the criminally insane, he felt at first a huge sense of relief. At last, he thought, he was being given the opportunity to pay for his crime. As time passed, however, he had the feeling that he was not paying enough. Day by day his feelings of guilt increased until one day he took a horrible step—he plunged his right arm into the huge propellers of a hospital washing machine. The limb was mangled beyond repair, but, oddly enough, no sooner had the patient lost the use of his arm than he recovered his sanity. One day he was a man with a serious mental illness and the normal number of arms, and the next he was a one-armed but mentally normal individual.

Clearly something had happened in the deep recesses of his unconscious mind. The man felt that by mutilating himself he had somehow atoned for the death of his son. He had paid, and paid dearly, for what he had done, and now he was free to resume a normal life.

In their self-loathing, some people go even further than that. For them the "one way left" is that ultimate in self-rejection—suicide.

An official of the World Health Organization reported recently that each day a thousand people throughout the world commit self-destruction. But equally serious, he said, is the fact that ten times that number—ten thousand people per day—*try* to take their own lives but fail in the attempt.

Why do people try to commit suicide? For all kinds of reasons. An unhappy love affair, chronic illness, public disgrace, economic problems, imitation, revenge, a sense of futility (plenty to live *on*, perhaps, but nothing to live *for*)—these are some of the causes of attempted self-destruction.

Undoubtedly though, underlying more than one of those causes, if not a cause in itself, is self-hatred. Again and again people seek to destroy themselves simply because they cannot stand themselves. Self-loathing can lead to self-destruction.

Fortunately most of us do not go nearly that far. Our self-dislike is much less acute and our self-hurt much less sudden and total—and certainly much less obvious. In our unhappiness with ourselves we punish ourselves, yes, but unconsciously, without even being aware of what we are doing.

We may, for example, smoke or drink too much and in so doing subject ourselves to all kinds of woes, to everything, in fact, from a hoarse throat to the d.t.'s.

We may join the ranks of the accident-prone, the people who incur one injury after another, an amazing assortment of mishaps, with most of those injuries being actually the result of self-punitive behavior on the part of a person deficient in self-appreciation—even though the person himself does not recognize that. A man so thoroughly dislikes himself, let us say, that he unconsciously "arranges" to punish himself by tripping over some trifling object and breaking his leg. Highly im-

3

probable? Perhaps so. But according to the authorities these things happen.

We may become workaholics, toiling morning, noon, and night, seven days a week, with the muddleheaded intention of, on the one hand, improving our worth and, on the other, driving ourselves into an early grave.

We may commit some senseless crime simply because, at a deep level, we want to be caught and punished. We actually invite others to inflict on us the punishment we feel we deserve.

We may become martyrs, working our fingers to the bone and ourselves to death in the service of other people or some worthy cause and, thereby, in the murky depths of our unconscious minds, somehow legitimizing our self-destruction.

We may take all kinds of foolish risks and, in the process, invite the self-damage or even self-annihilation we feel is our due. It has been said of a celebrated escape artist that "almost every stunt staged by Houdini represented a form of pseudo-suicide."[1] Erich Fromm made much the same point when he termed excessive risk-running "the courage of nihilism, a willingness to throw life away because one is incapable of living it."[2]

In point of fact there are a great many ways in which, in their dislike of themselves, people make life enormously difficult and even impossible for themselves. Over and over again, in every way imaginable, some perfectly obvious and some profoundly subtle, people express self-hatred by denying, avoiding, humiliating, punishing, and destroying themselves.

"Of all the infirmities we have," said Montaigne, "the most savage is to despise our being."[3] It was a perceptive comment, and one with which it is hard to disagree.

*　　*　　*

Our self-hatred would not be quite so serious if its target were only the self, but, unfortunately, that is never the case. Always the hatred includes others as well. In a nutshell, the two hatreds—the hatred of self and hatred of others—always go hand in hand. In fact, whenever we see someone who in one way or another is lashing out at other people, we can be sure of this: deep down, he hates himself.

I remember talking with a woman who had been a nun and who was savagely critical of the Roman Catholic church. In the hour or so we were together, she went on and on, sometimes angry and sometimes on the verge of tears, denouncing the church in the most scathing terms. She had absolutely no use, she said, for its authoritarianism, its archaic style, and its utter indifference to human need. But most of all she deplored the rampant immorality that, according to her, prevailed between priests and nuns. I had no idea, she said, of all the dark doings that went on behind ecclesiastical walls.

As the torrent of condemnation went on, I found myself becoming more and more suspicious. "The lady doth protest too much," I said to myself. "There's something wrong here. Surely the churches aren't all *that* bad."

As it turned out, those suspicions were well-founded. A few months later I learned that the ex-nun had been dismissed from her order for the very failing that she had so vehemently condemned in others—she had been involved in an illicit relationship with a priest who subsequently had also left the church.

Again and again we see the same thing. In the teenage delinquent who vandalizes the neighborhood, in the evangelical preacher who is happiest when loudly denouncing a Godless society, in the surly policeman who positively delights in cracking down with the full weight of the law on those guilty of even the most minor misdemeanors, in the stand-up comic whose "humor" is basically a savage put-down of the straight-man partner—in all these people and many more we see a hatred of others which points directly to a hatred of self.

In the words of Grace Stuart: "The point to be made is just this: that a loving attitude to others and a hating attitude to the self cannot possibly be nurtured together. They may appear to exist together, but if the self-hatred is real, then the love of others will prove to be a mask, covering hatred of them, too. Similarly, when hatred (often seen as selfishness or indifference) of others appears to go with love of self, the 'love' will mask self-hatred."[4]

* * *

Only in this century have scientists learned that when ailing infants are hospitalized in hygienic and comfortable surroundings, and when they are given the best of food and medical treatment—but nothing more—the great majority of them, far from recovering, go from bad to worse. The explanation for their deterioration and death? It is simple: no love. Without people to cuddle them and coo over them, these love-starved babies are unable to go on living.

We adults, too, cannot live without love. We can *exist* without it, yes, but we certainly cannot *live*, with all that the word implies. Without love we are left with a largely meaningless existence, one sadly devoid of any deep and abiding satisfaction.

Most of us recognize that fact; we recognize how much we need the love of others. But what we do not so commonly recognize is that it is equally essential to love ourselves.

At home, and at church and school, I remember, I was consistently exposed to the great moral and spiritual truths by which men have been guided for centuries past. But oddly enough there is one ideal that I missed, one that either was never presented or was presented but, unfortunately, went right by me. It was the ideal of self-love. I was often told that it is our duty to love our neighbors, but I cannot recall even a single time in the early years of my life when someone tried to impress upon me the importance of loving ourselves. As a matter of fact, I was well along in adulthood before I became aware of the fact that, while it is important to love our fellowmen, it is just as important to love ourselves.

I suspect though that my experience is not unique. My guess is that the great majority of us go through our childhood and youth without the slightest inkling of the value of self-love.

The omission is strange, especially in view of the fact that down through the centuries some of the most eminent figures in history have stressed the importance of self-love. Plato, Aristotle, Augustine, Luther, Spinoza, Kant, Dewey, and Sartre are only a few of the philosophers and saints who emphasized that one of our primary obligations is to love ourselves.

In the Great Commandment, which sums up a person's whole religious duty, Jesus too stated that self-love is all-important: "You shall love the Lord your God with all your heart, and with all your soul, and with all your strength, and with all your mind; and your neighbor *as yourself.*"[5]

Teachers in other religions—Hindus, Taoists, Buddhists, Confucianists, Moslems, and Jews—say much the same thing: human salvation is impossible apart from the love of self.

Anthropologists point out that when a tribe of people loses its self-respect, it can also lose its will to live. Men and women stop reproducing or simply lie down and die beside streams full of fish. It would appear that, for some people, life without self-appreciation is not even worth living.

Psychologists too maintain that self-love is absolutely fundamental to human well-being. Without a sense of personal worth, they say, one cannot function in a normal way; one becomes instead a prime candidate for some kind of crippling neurosis.

Alfred Adler, a giant in the realm of psychiatry, parted company from Freud in stating that a person's strongest desire is not for sexual gratification but for self-esteem. "The supreme law [of life]," he said, "is this: the sense of the worth of the self shall not be allowed to be diminished."[6]

We begin life, said Adler, in a state of total inferiority. Small and feeble, we are completely at the mercy of the powers that be—our mothers and fathers, aunts, uncles, teachers, and all the others who make up the adult world. In most cases these dominant figures are kind and gentle people, but still they *rule*; they are wielders of enormous power and, as such, the objects of our profound resentment. Deep down, we are most unhappy with our subjection, and we long for the day when we will be on an equal or superior footing.

Remember how, as small children, we used to fight our way to the top of some little eminence and chant, "I'm the king of the castle, and you're the dirty rascals," only to be deposed by a playmate who would then become "king of the castle"?

Well, there it is, the desire for status and self-esteem, which, according to Adler, remains the most powerful urge in our lives for as long as we live.

* * *

In literally hundreds of ways, we minister to our need for self-esteem. We drive a big car, amass large sums of money, or, in Don Juan fashion, achieve one sexual conquest after another. We write a book, outperform others on the golf course, or step up to some prestigious position. We devote ourselves to good works, acquire an advanced academic degree, prod our children to great heights of performance, or wangle our way into some exclusive social group. In all these ways and a host of others we say to ourselves, "I'm not a nonentity. I'm *somebody*, a significant person."

However, in spite of all our striving and self-reassurance, our self-esteem remains a fragile quality, something in need of repeated reinforcement. Harry Emerson Fosdick was right on target when he said, "Because of our inside information about ourselves and the mortifying situations which outwardly we face, every person confronts the lurking devil of self-contempt. That is one reason why we welcome praise so eagerly; the approval of our friends helps to lift us above our low self-estimate. That is why we are so pleased by position, office, and prestige; they reestablish our uncertain self-confidence."[7]

It is for this reason too that day in and day out we keep affirming our essential worth. In *Requiem for a Heavyweight* Anthony Quinn played one of his greatest roles. A battered pug, doomed to eventual annihilation in the ring, he kept reiterating both to himself and to others that, after all, he was the "*fifth*-ranking contender for the heavyweight crown." We do much the same thing: in a world that so often humiliates us we work ceaselessly at reinforcing our fragile self-esteem.

It is not going too far to say that scores of times each day and quite unconsciously we call to our minds those glowing little episodes that enhance our feeling of self-worth. The successful business transaction, the boss's approval, the well-told joke that evoked uproarious laughter, the heartwarming compliment, the beautifully executed performance, and the subtle but unmistakable invitation to illicit romance—all these minor but delectable triumphs we keep reviewing over and over again as fuel for our self-esteem.

We do not, of course, have the same control over our thought processes when night comes and we fall asleep, and it is then, in our dreams—or, rather, nightmares— that the negative images sometimes emerge and flood our minds, with the result that we feel dirty and ashamed, or horribly threatened and utterly helpless, or out of control and headed for certain destruction. Eventually we waken, rigid with tension and emotionally exhausted but immensely relieved ("Whew, I'm glad it was only a dream!"), and immediately we set about restoring our mental equilibrium.

In the daytime too every attack on our self-esteem tends to be followed by some kind of rehabilitative action. A little girl, for example, is scolded by her mother. What does she do next? She heads straight for the family's dog, a big, gentle, good-natured animal which lavishes upon her his undiluted affection—balm for her poor, bruised little ego. A man, again, receives a severe tongue-lashing from his boss. Humiliated and hurt, he turns to his wife who through sheer love restores his shattered self-respect.

*   *   *

Long ago, according to Ovid's version of the Greek legend, there was a nymph, Liriope, who was ravished by the river-god Cephisus. Months later, Liriope gave birth to an extraordinarily beautiful child, a boy named Narcissus. As the years passed, the boy's beauty reached even more awesome proportions. By the time he was sixteen, many youths and maidens sought his love. But, for all his beauty, Narcissus was an extremely cold person, utterly incapable of returning the love he was offered.

People suffered from Narcissus' rejection of them, but no one more than the nymph Echo, who had fallen passionately in love with the youth. Typically, Narcissus fled from Echo, crying out that he would rather be dead than in any way subject to her. Thus rejected, Echo pined away until finally there was nothing left of her except her voice.

Echo was not the only one hurt by Narcissus. Scores of people, young men as well as the nymphs, were spurned by Narcissus with the most icy disdain. Some were heartbroken, some exceedingly bitter.

In the end, as it turned out, it was one of these rejected suitors who was responsible for Narcissus' downfall. Praying to the gods for vengeance on Narcissus, the suitor petitioned, "So may he love and not gain the thing he loves!" Nemesis, one of the gods, heard this prayer, felt that it deserved to be answered, and ordained accordingly that Narcissus should lie down to drink from a woodland pool so clear and still that it would provide him with a flawless reflection of his own physical perfection.

Looking into the pool, Narcissus was "smitten by the sight of the beautiful form." He was, in fact, so captivated by his own image, mirrored there in the dark depths of the pool, that he could not tear himself away. At the water's edge he stayed, until finally he laid "his weary head on the green grass" and death "sealed the eyes that marvelled at their master's beauty."

Even in Hades, says the legend, Narcissus, as self-absorbed as ever, "kept gazing on his image in the Stygian pool." More and more, however, this beautiful but self-obsessed young man, once an object of the most extreme resentment and envy, became an object of pity. Naiads and dryads, and even Echo, now only a voice, paid him the tribute of their mourning, which so touched the gods that finally they transformed the wasted body into a beautiful flower.

Narcissus was, of course, only a mythical figure, but that figure has many counterparts in daily life. Probably all of us know someone who has narcissistic tendencies, someone so obsessed with himself that he gives almost no thought to anyone or anything else. Everything is seen in reference to himself, and always his thoughts keep coming back to himself.

In one of the cartoon strips in his delightful *Peanuts* series, Charles Schulz has Charlie Brown chiding Lucy for her incessant self-centeredness. "You know," says Charlie, "you talk about yourself all the time! You may

13

not realize it, but all you ever say is, 'I' 'I' 'I' 'I' 'I'!!" Lucy's response: "I?"[8]

People like Lucy are not at all uncommon—people whose sole interest in life is themselves, people whose self-preoccupation stretches our tolerance to its very limits. But just as narcissism can be a highly distasteful quality so also can it be a strangely attractive quality.

One afternoon I was with my wife in the dress department of a large downtown store when I happened to notice one of the most striking, sartorially elegant and perfectly beautiful men I had ever seen. He too was standing around while his wife searched for some clothing. He was not, however, merely standing. He was *posing*. Tall and slim, with perfect aquiline features and dressed in the height of fashion, he was leaning gracefully on a furled umbrella while, all around, saleswomen and shoppers alike were discreetly but quite noticeably goggling at this entrancing creature.

Obviously a narcissist, a man who had spent countless hours in paying homage to his own reflection, he was also a man who commanded massive interest on the part of other people. Like many narcissists, he was the center of attention, not only his own attention but that of others as well.

Freud recognized this phenomenon when he said, "It seems very evident that one person's narcissism has a great attraction for those others who have renounced part of their own narcissism and are seeking after object-love; the charm of a child lies to a great extent in his narcissism, just as does the charm of certain animals which seem not to concern themselves about us, such as cats and the large beasts of prey."[9]

The fact is, though, that the narcissist is a deficient person, someone who was emotionally deprived as a child and who has never fully recovered. In the very first few weeks of his life, a child begins reaching out toward the people and objects around him. Inevitably, he meets with certain responses, and those responses largely determine what kind of person he eventually becomes. If he meets with acceptance, tenderness, and love he feels encouraged to move out even further; not only his confidence is increased but also his capacity for love. If, however, as a result of those first, fumbling, exploratory efforts he finds himself lost, rejected, or hurt, he tends to call a halt to outreach of any kind and to turn inward for the satisfaction of his emotional needs. In other words, he develops narcissistic tendencies that may prevail for the rest of his life.

* * *

All too many of us have the idea that self-love is synonymous with narcissism. As we see it, the self-loving person is someone who is absolutely full of himself, someone who is forever dwelling on the subject of himself and whose chief concern is "the great God I." That, however, is narcissism, not self-love.

The difference between the two? Well, narcissism is indeed egocentricity or self-centeredness, or, as a Christian might put it, pride.

In the popular view, pride is expressed in a certain haughtiness and arrogance, in a lordly and condescending manner. From the Christian point of view, however, pride—the cardinal sin—is not so much a matter of a superior attitude as it is of self-centeredness. Pride, says the Christian, is seen in the person who has put himself at the center of his own little universe and made himself the object of all his interest and devotion—the person who has in effect displaced God in favor of himself, setting himself up as his own God. That, for the Christian, is pride.

Others—Erich Fromm, for example—equate narcissism with selfishness, which, they say, is not even distantly related to self-love. We have the idea, many of us, that selfishness and self-love are one and the same thing, but according to Fromm, that is not the case at all. In point of fact, the two are total opposites, poles apart.

A selfish person, says Fromm, is one who is all wrapped up in himself, so preoccupied with his own interests and needs that he gives little thought to anyone or anything unrelated to those needs.

Why this obsession with self? Why is it that some people's attention is given almost entirely to themselves? Basically, because they are extremely insecure people—so insecure, in fact, that they need all the attention they can get not only from others but also from themselves. Most people are able to relinquish responsibility for themselves: trust themselves, take themselves for granted, and, having done that, forget themselves, move out of themselves and away from themselves, and lose (and thereby find) themselves in all kinds of extra-personal interests. Some people, however, are incapable of doing that. Because at a deep level they are afraid that their untended selves would somehow collapse and be lost, these people are, so to speak, forever fluttering around themselves, supporting and reinforcing themselves. We say that they are selfish or self-centered people, and so they are. But they are also people who deserve pity, not censure, for in a very real sense they are prisoners of their own anxiety.

I remember being in deep trouble at one point in my life and driving hundreds of miles in order to talk with a man who, I was convinced, could be immensely helpful. I drove nearly all night and, early in the morning, arrived at his place—a weary, haggard, and desperately confused individual. But I was hopeful. At last, I thought, I had found someone who could help me get everything straightened out. As it happened, though, I did not find the understanding I expected. I found, rather, a man who simply would not listen. Over and over again I set out to explain my predicament, only to have him cut me short and begin telling me all about his own situation, with the emphasis on his glowing successes and even more glowing expectations. Finally I left and headed for home feeling worse than ever. My original problem was still there, compounded now by a seething mix of disappointment, frustration, and rage. I must admit that even now, over twenty years later, I cannot recount the incident without feeling a twinge of bitterness. However, the problem has long since passed, and with it most of the resentment I once felt. I am not nearly so critical now of the man as I was twenty years ago because I see something now I did not see then. I see that I went to the wrong person—I went to someone who could not give me the support I needed because, basically, he had all he could do to support himself.

Unlike that man, the person who loves himself is a fundamentally secure person and therefore a self-disregarding and outgoing person. He is a man who is not easily threatened, a man who has the deep-down feeling that "everything is OK at home" and who, in that confidence, is able to dismiss himself, leave himself behind, and fully identify himself with the outside world. He is a man, moreover, who is relaxed, a man at peace with himself.

We tend to see love as a state of strong emotion. To love someone or something, as we see it, is to *care*, to feel deeply about that particular person or thing. Love is not calm, judicial, or detached. No, say we, love involves fervor, passion, and intensity.

What we need to see, though, is that love is not necessarily a matter of a lot of torrid emotion. Love can also be quiet, casual, matter-of-fact. Indeed, self-love is just that. The man who loves himself has few strong feelings about himself one way or another, at least few strong conscious feelings. Why this absence of emotion? Because he is a man who gives little thought to himself. He is an unself-conscious person.

A sign over the entrance to a children's clubhouse read, "Nobody act big, nobody act small, everybody act medium." In a sense, the man who loves himself acts "medium." He is an in-betweener. He does not on the one hand loathe and despise himself, and he does not on the other, like Narcissus, spend his life in perpetual self-adoration. A beautifully balanced person, the man who loves himself walks the middle way of self-forgetfulness.

In the words of Grace Stuart: "The true self-love does not feel like love to the lover; it feels, we may surmise, like peace. No more noticeable, when you have it, than is the rightness of good health. So, to the general eye it is precisely the self-loving person who seems not to love himself at all. For he is of his nature free from the attributes we decry as selfish, and his ability to love himself shows itself chiefly in the warmth, spontaneity and skill of his interest in persons and things outside of, and other than himself."[10]

Antoine de Saint-Exupéry used to speak of being one's own friend and, in so doing, put it in a nutshell: the person who loves himself is his own friend. He is not his own enemy, and he is not his own God. He is his own *friend.*

He is a person, therefore, who enjoys his own company. I know people who cannot stand being alone. For them an empty house or apartment presents an intolerable situation, a hell from which they must somehow escape—perhaps by going out, looking for company, or having people in, or perhaps by switching on the TV set, turning up the volume full blast, and in that way filling the place with the sound of actors, musicians, commentators, and other such substitute-friends. Unlike such people, however, the person who loves himself is not disquieted by solitude. He is a man who is at peace with himself, at home with himself, a man who is thoroughly comfortable with himself—so much so, in fact, that if need be he can spend some time all by himself, perfectly content with his own company. He is, of course, no hermit. He thoroughly enjoys the company of other people, but at the same times he does not crave their company. He is not excessively dependent on his fellow-men for companionship and fun because, basically, he has a good friend, one of his best friends, right in himself.

It follows that, as his own friend, the man who loves himself treats himself kindly. Unlike those who dislike themselves he does not punish or neglect himself or in one way or another try to destroy himself. Rather, to himself too he accords a certain "reverence for life." Just as, unconsciously, almost intuitively, he sees others as beings to be cherished, protected, and served, so also he sees himself. Just as, in his dealings with his friends especially, he is gentle, tolerant, generous, and understanding, so also he is in his dealings with himself. He is essentially a kind person, kind to others, yes, and also kind to himself.

*   *   *

Every day the news media tell of the extent to which hatred and violence prevail in society. Teenage delinquents vandalize their neighbor's property; terrorists highjack planes and hold innocent people hostage; previously mild-mannered individuals suddenly go berserk and spray bullets into crowded areas; small children are beaten black and blue, in some cases beaten to death, by enraged parents; muggers, rapists, and murderers roam our cities' streets; and whole nations are sundered by civil war.

All in all it is an ugly, depressing picture, and one which says in no uncertain terms that our society's most crying need is for love. We need new energy sources. We need to control the population explosion, to call a halt to environmental pollution, and to provide for a more equitable sharing of the earth's resources. But in, through, and beyond all these things, we need love.

The point, however, is this: we can create this ever so necessary climate of love only to the extent that we love ourselves.

A number of people have the idea that love of self and love of others are incompatible. The more we love ourselves, they say, the less we love others, and conversely, the more we love others, the less we love ourselves.

Freud, for instance, argued in very quantitative terms that man has only "a certain amount of capacity to love"[11] and that when we spend our love on others, we have just that much less left for ourselves. Others have said much the same thing, but in reverse, by stating that the love of self is always expressed at the expense of the love of others. We dare not, they say, love ourselves too much, for to do that is to short-change our neighbors. In truth, however, the two loves—love of self and love of others—are basically one and, as such, are always *jointly* cultivated. The more we love ourselves the more we love others, and vice versa.

Said Meister Eckhart, the German mystic, "If you love yourself, you love everybody else as you do yourself. As long as you love another person less than you love yourself, you will not really succeed in loving yourself, but if you love all alike including yourself, you will love them as one person and that person is both God and man. Thus he is a great and righteous person who, loving himself, loves all others equally."[12]

Søren Kierkegaard expressed the same truth in even more striking terms: "If anyone, therefore, will not learn from Christianity to love himself in the right way, then neither can he love his neighbor. He may perhaps . . . cling to one of several other human beings, but this is by no means loving one's neighbor. To love oneself in the right way, and to love one's neighbor, are absolutely analogous concepts, and are at the bottom one and the same."[13]

* * *

But now the question: is self-love a gift or an achievement? Is it a blessing, given to this person but denied to that, or is it a quality cultivated more by some people and less by others?

Actually self-love is neither one nor the other; it is *both*. On the one hand, it is a virtue that is almost native to some people—to Goethe, for example. On the other hand, it is an attribute that some men and women earn only with considerable difficulty and over a period of many years.

Which raises a further question: to the extent that self-love is acquired, *how* is it acquired?

The answer to that question (to be spelled out in the chapters which follow) is this: *we cultivate self-love by cultivating its three components—self-being, self-acceptance, and self-discipline.*

In other words, as we go on and on *being* ourselves, *accepting* ourselves, and *disciplining* ourselves we more and more become genuinely loving people, individuals who love themselves and, in loving themselves, love others as well.

2.

BEING OURSELVES:

The First Step in Loving Ourselves

Self-being, one of self-love's essential elements, is apparently less in evidence now than it was years ago. It seems that people today are largely lacking in the rich individuality that was characteristic of an earlier generation.

I remember an evening in which a distinguished older man, raised on the island of Cape Breton, regaled us with stories of some of the people he had known as a boy. Plain, frugal, God-fearing people, a high percentage of these Cape Bretoners were also amazingly eccentric. "Characters," our narrator termed them, and so they were—men and women of magnificent individuality, people who were not in the least reticent about being themselves.

"But people aren't like that anymore, even in Cape Breton," lamented the ex-native. "Most of us nowadays are afraid to be ourselves."

I remember, too, Edith Sitwell's delightful book, *English Eccentrics*, in which she tells of some of the men and women whose odd behavior was outstanding even in an age renowned for its flourishing individualism.

One of the people of whom Dame Sitwell wrote, John Mytton, squire of Halston, near Shrewsbury, was born on September 30, 1796, and died at the age of 38 of "too much foolishness, too much wretchedness, and too much brandy."[1] Prior to that unhappy event, however, he led a life of astounding eccentricity.

Perhaps because he brought a little excitement and color into their lives John Mytton was always appreciated by the common people, who permitted him to take some extraordinary liberties. When, for example, he was returning from a hunt, chilled to the marrow, he would not hesitate to invite himself and his favorite horse Baronet into a cottager's house and ask that a big fire be lit to warm the two of them. Horse and master would then lounge side by side by the fire until they were warm enough to set out for home.

Perhaps, though, the squire's most unforgettable performance had to do with a case of the hiccups, his own. Unable to dispel them, John Mytton came to the odd conclusion that a good way to get rid of them would be to frighten them away by setting his nightshirt on fire, which, using a lighted candle, he proceeded to do. Fortunately, a couple of intrepid bystanders managed to rip off the flaming garment. But, as far as the squire was concerned, it was an eminently successful endeavor: the hiccups had disappeared completely.

Dr. Martin van Butchell was a London dentist who wore a long gray beard and rode a white pony painted with purple, peony-sized spots. Sad to say, Dr. van

Butchell lost his wife in January, 1775. Reluctant to part with her, he had her body embalmed. The mummy was kept in a case with a glass lid and curtains and was introduced to visitors as "my dear departed." Inevitably, word of this intriguing spectacle got around and visitors became more and more numerous. In fact, there were so many of these sightseers that finally the good doctor was forced to place in the *St. James's Chronicle* of October 31, 1775 a notice which read: "Van Butchell, not wishing to be unpleasantly circumstanced, and wishing to convince some good minds they have been misinformed, acquaints the Curious, no stranger can see his embalmed wife unless (by a friend personally) introduced by himself, any day between nine and one, Sundays excepted."[2] Eventually the man remarried. But, as it turned out, the new Mrs. van Butchell took such strong exception to the presence of the "dear departed" that her husband was forced to arrange for a suitable burial.

Jemmy Hirst, a stout, hearty man with a florid complexion, was a tanner who retired from business with a sizeable fortune. One of the interesting items in the ex-tanner's house was a coffin which, thoughtfully, he had bought for his own interment and which meanwhile he used as a liquor cabinet in the dining room.

Mr. Hirst's favorite pursuit was hunting. But, because he was not fond of horses, he went shooting "mounted on the back of a bull of ample proportions and uncertain temper, whilst for pointers, he made use of the services of a crowd of vivacious and sagacious pigs, all of whom answered to their names, and did their duty irreproachably."[3] Legend has it, further, that this unusual gentleman sometimes rode with the Badsworth hounds. All the hunters were dressed and mounted in the usual fashion with the exception of the ex-tanner, who could be seen thundering over the meadows astride his enormous bull.

Hirst lived to the ripe age of ninety and went to his rest in typically colorful fashion. Having been emptied of its alcoholic contents so that it could accommodate its owner, the coffin was carried to the grave by eight stout widows, who were followed by a large procession of sporting men, all stepping along to the accompaniment of a lively march played on a bagpipe and fiddle.

Several generations have passed since that "golden age of English eccentrics." But in our time and society, too, there are those whose life-style is, to say the least, highly unusual.

An Arkansas woman has her house filled with uncaged birds, scores of them, which flutter and swoosh all over the place. It costs her $200 a month to feed them—not to mention the cleaning expenses.

A wealthy Kansan who likes going places in his car but dislikes driving has found, as he sees it, the perfect solution: he has his Rolls Royce loaded aboard a railroad flatcar, positions himself behind the wheel of the Rolls, and there, enthroned in solitary splendor, travels all over the place.

John Zink, the larger-than-life owner of a 10,000-acre ranch near Tulsa, used to greet guests by firing a revolver into the overhead beams of his baronial office but cut out the practice when a ricocheting bullet came within a hair's breadth of felling his secretary.

One evening, as he was entertaining a Supreme Court justice, Zink enlivened the proceedings by turning loose a pack of hound dogs and a raccoon in the middle of dinner. He probably did not do much for his guest's digestion, but it certainly must have made for an unforgettable meal.

It seems, though, that these flamboyant characters are increasingly scarce. Gone, apparently, are the days when there were all kinds of men and women who, in their towering individualism, were bright flashes of color in the human landscape. Gone are those days in favor of a gray, homogeneous society in which thousands upon thousands of people are scarcely distinguishable from one another.

"But," someone may argue, "look at all the long-haired youth. Look at the multiplicity of new life-styles and standards of behavior. Look at all the modes of dress, and undress, on display on the streets of any great city, the incredible profusion of strange political groups and bizarre religious cults. Look at the literally millions of people who are all doing their own thing. A conformist society? We are anything but!"

A closer look at the situation might suggest, though, that the behavior patterns are not nearly so profuse as they seem. Granted there are a great many people who do not conform to the usual standards. But in their own way they too are conformists, people who fall in line not with cultural but with countercultural norms. Which is to say, the bearded young rebel, devoted to soft drugs, indiscriminate sex, and the writings of Eastern sages, is in his own way just as much a conformist as his staid, middle-aged stockbroker father. One conforms to the standards of his peer-group no less than the other.

What we are witnessing, it seems, is not so much a plethora of life-styles as a polarization of cultures. On the one hand, there are all the people who make up the conventional culture—the solid, respectable people who live conservatively and are firm believers in patriotism, God, industry, thrift, and, in general, all "the good old-fashioned virtues." On the other hand, there is the more youthful group which constitutes the counterculture—the people whose values and life-style all bespeak a wholesale rejection of the Establishment, the people who tend to be judged, especially by their elders, as radical, rebellious, immoral, and in many ways a serious threat to the status quo. Granted there are a number of people who do not fall into either camp and there is a fair amount of diversity within each of the two camps. But by and large, overriding this diversity, there is a striking conformity—on the one hand the conformity of the right and on the other the conformity of the left.

Why this widespread mass-mindedness? Why is it that more and more we are becoming "a nation of sheep?"

There is no simple answer to the question, but certainly one of the reasons for our herd-behavior is the influence of the mass media.

Generations ago a great many people spent their entire lives in comparatively small and isolated agrarian communities. In those days people did not know what was happening even in the next county, much less on the other side of the world. As a result of this isolationism there was, inevitably, an extraordinary cultural diversity. People in one community spoke differently, dressed differently, and worked, played, and worshipped differently, in fact did all kinds of things differently from the people in a community only a few miles away. But that is not the case today. We live today in a huge "global village," a world in which, as a result of an amazingly sophisticated system of communications, we are very much aware of people thousands of miles away and very much influenced by their attitudes and actions.

Yves St. Laurent comes out in Paris with a new look in women's fashions. In a matter of hours his creations are being shown by television all over the world, and in mere weeks they are accepted by literally millions of women in Anchorage, Alaska, in Sydney, Australia, and in any number of places in between.

In a thousand and one ways both by accident and by design the mass media are responsible for shaping and standardizing our behavior.

It can be argued, of course, that a certain amount of regimentation is essential to the smooth functioning of any complex society. If, for instance, on a particular day in the city of San Francisco everyone were to indulge his or her every fancy and whim, if people were to go to work when and if they felt like it and on the job do whatever they pleased, if everyone were to abandon all social restraints and let self-expression run absolutely rampant, the result would be sheer chaos.

There must be a certain amount of social restriction. But, necessary though it may be to some degree, conformity can be, and usually is, carried too far. Most of us are too much "other-directed" for our own good.

* * *

When we allow ourselves to be "conformed to this world"[4] one of the greatest disservices we do ourselves is that we deny our God-given individuality.

We are, each of us, absolutely unique. Of the billions of people on the face of this planet no two are exactly alike.

The police recognize this fact and they take full advantage of it. As one man put it, "Individual differences are what police detection is all about." Here, for example, is a criminal, identified by his fingerprints, unlike any others in the entire world. Here, too, is a law-breaker who is tracked down by bloodhounds, animals which have a superb sense of smell and which are guided by a man's characteristic odor. Again, individual differences.

It is an amazing thought: no two of us alike. Cars, radios, cameras, and a host of other mechanical items are all mass produced but not mankind. Our genetic

31

structure, our brains, incredible in their complexity, in fact everything about us is distinctive, unique.

Not long ago a friend said to me, "I saw your twin—someone exactly like you." The fact is that I have no twin; nor have you. We are essentially unique, you and I, "one of a kind," and, in our uniqueness, of infinite worth.

It follows that when we allow our uniqueness to be submerged, when we yield to social compulsions and become like millions of others, gray, anonymous people, we lose something of our intrinsic value and, in a very real sense, deny our Creator's intention—we undo what he has done.

In reminding us of our obligation to be ourselves, Martin Buber said: "Every person born into this world represents something new, something that never existed before, something original and unique. It is the duty of every person . . . to know . . . that there has never been anyone like him in the world, for if there had been someone like him, there would have been no need for him to be in the world. Every single man is a new thing in the world and is called upon to fulfill his particularity in this world."[5]

Indeed, right here, in our very uniqueness, are grounds for self-love. In the words of William Cole: "The proper appreciation of one's worth is to be derived not from a sense of superiority but from a recognition of uniqueness. No one can be sure of being always the best at anything, but one can be certain eternally of being different. In all the eons of time stretching behind and before, there never has been nor will be anyone exactly like any individual self. No two snowflakes, grains of sand, leaves, or blades of grass are ever exactly alike. Even in identical twins the fingerprints are different. Every human being brings into being with him potentialities, gifts, and abilities which no one else can ever realize or bring to fruition and actuality."[6]

*   *   *

People of all ages experience frustration and, as a result of that frustration, anger and resentment.

A small child, for example, is prevented again and again from doing what he wants. He tries to crawl down the basement stairs, he tries to get at the delicate glass objects on an endtable, he tries to empty the contents of his cereal bowl over his head, and in every instance a voice says "No" and strong hands interfere with his plans. It is no wonder that at times the small adventurer is livid with rage.

As the child grows older, he experiences the same thing, one frustration after another. "Jimmy," called a mother to her small son who was ominously quiet in another part of the house, "whatever you're doing, stop it!"

Harry Emerson Fosdick once told of a friend who was on a train when a mother came aboard with her small son in tow and took the seat directly in front of the man. One of the woman's first words to her son was "Don't." But that was just the beginning. By the count

33

of the man behind, in a mere hour and a half the mother said "Don't" to her child no less than fifty-nine times!

How often a child is told, "Stop it!" "Don't!" "Cut it out!" How often he is restrained by sheer force from following through on his natural inclinations. Again, it is no wonder that there are times when, purple with rage, he stamps his feet and shouts at his parents, "I hate you, I hate you!" Who can blame him?

In time the small boy becomes an adolescent, and perhaps it is then that his frustrations are most acute. He wants to stay up later at night, he wants freer access to the family car, he wants to wear casual clothes to semiformal occasions—the list of his unfulfilled wants could be extended almost ad infinitum—and, denied these things, he becomes sullen, uncommunicative, and even downright rebellious, a profoundly resentful person and a problem to all concerned, including himself.

We may not have had such a difficult time in adolescence, you and I, but there were countless occasions when we too were prevented from doing what we wanted. Eventually, however, we emerged from that aggravating period, and now here we are, grown men and women. That is not to say that the pressure is off. Far from it. For even as adults we are under constant pressure to behave in certain ways.

I remember seeing a movie about a young banker who elected to grow a beard. In most situations a decision like that would not cause the slightest stir. But in this case the young man's ultraconservative superiors were absolutely outraged. "A bearded bank employee," they fumed. "We've never heard of such a thing! It's totally unacceptable. The beard will have to go. Either that or its owner will."

Most of us are not bankers. But whatever we are we cannot escape the pressure to conform to certain behavioral standards. In matters of morals and speech, in matters of manners and dress, in fact in the whole matter of "style," we are under constant pressure to blend inconspicuously into the social background.

Furthermore, to refuse to submit to those pressures, to go one's own way, stepping to "the sound of a different drummer," is inevitably to invite trouble, that is, criticism, ridicule, disgrace, or even worse.

There is a considerable difference, though, between the kind of social pressure we experienced as children and the kind we experience as adults. In those days the pressure was clear and direct. We were told quite explicitly "Do this" or "Do that," and generally, even though most unhappily, we did it. But not so today. Now the pressure, while it is no less real, is much more subtle.

There is a difference, too, between the ways in which children and adults are punished. When I was about ten years old my best friend and I were competing to see who could build up the biggest stamp collection. One day, hoping to add to our collections in a substantial way, we decided to take a fling at shoplifting. The target was a downtown store and the caper went off without a hitch. But for days thereafter my conscience made life sheer hell. However, as it generally does, the truth finally came out; my friend's small brother leaked the news of our misbehavior. My parents, understandably, were most upset. After I had been spanked and marched down to the store to return the stamps, I was sent to bed without any supper. Also, my stamp collection was confiscated. What happened to it I was never told. (I do know, though, that the next day my parents behaved as if nothing had happened. All was apparently forgiven and forgotten.)

I mention the incident because most children are, at least occasionally, dealt with in much the same way. From time to time they are subjected to some kind of corporal punishment.

As adults we do not have to undergo that kind of treatment. No one says to us, "If you don't behave yourself, I'll paddle your bottom." However, we are threatened with another, far more devastating kind of punishment, namely rejection.

I think, for example, of the housewife who would like nothing more than to be a liberated woman. With her children now in their teens, she could go back to the university or go out and get a job. But the problem is her husband. A typical member of the old school, in fact a petty tyrant, he believes that a woman's place is in the home—cooking, cleaning, ironing, mending, and, above all, looking after her husband. As he sees it, a woman's chief concern should be ministering to her husband's needs, and heaven help her if she doesn't.

Never, as it happens, does the husband articulate his position in simple, forthright terms. But the threat is still there, implicitly. His wife has been given to understand quite clearly that she had better stay in line or else. Or else what? Rejection, which might mean, as more than once it has in the past, the refusal of the husband to speak to his wife for days on end or which might even mean the termination of the marriage.

In a very real sense, the woman is a prisoner, too afraid of her husband to run the risk of being her own person and, without being aware of it, deeply resentful of her husband, herself, and the whole situation.

I think, too, of the countless men who are in jobs in which they feel hopelessly frustrated and stifled. In the very depths of their being, these men long to be individuals, uniquely themselves, not just tiny cogs, identical to many others and going through the same mindless motions over and over again in some massive bureaucracy. But for them that kind of freedom and individuality are not possible. Tradition, convention, the market, and, above all, their superiors combine to say to them in no uncertain terms, "Remember, you're not indispensable. If you value your position, and if you don't want to be out on the street, you'll do as you're told, and no questions asked." It is no wonder that within so many of these men, smouldering away, there is profound resentment. They hate the system and, more than that, they hate themselves for so meekly acceding to the system's demands.

In some cases we fail to recognize our dependency and consequent resentment, thereby adding to the problem.

Several years ago I was deeply unhappy in my work as a minister. On the face of it I had every reason for gratitude. I was young and healthy, had a fine family, and was serving a large congregation which occupied a beautiful neo-Gothic building in Montreal, one of Canada's most colorful cities. But still I was a most unhappy person without really knowing why. Of course, there were the usual reasons, the ones voiced by ministerial malcontents all over the place. I resented the long hours, the countless meetings, and the relentless demands of the pulpit, having to come up with something fresh and stimulating Sunday after Sunday, week in and week out all year long. I resented the ultraconservatism of some church members, the indifference of the general public, and the essential loneliness of the ministry, the gulf there often is between the "man of God" and the man on the street. But somehow I could not put my finger on the real problem, nor of course on the solution.

One day my wife and I were talking about the situation. Rather, *I* was talking. Phyl did not do much but listen quietly and understandingly while I went on and on, pouring out my troubles. Then it happened—in the course of my monologue, I used the term "passive-dependent." Those two words stopped me dead in my tracks, set me thinking, and sparked a tremendous insight. For the first time I saw that at a deep, unconscious level I had been resenting my congregation. Naturally, I had pretended to all concerned, including myself, that I loved them. But in plain fact I had come close to hating them. Why? Because I had been overly dependent on them. I had, of course, been financially dependent on them—after all it was they who were paying my salary. But more than that, I had been emotionally dependent on them. I had seen them as my chief source of acceptance and approval. In short I had looked to them for *security*, both financial and emotional. My feelings toward them had been, in fact, much like those of an unhappy adolescent toward his parents. I had loved them, yes, to a degree. But I had also resented them and longed to be free of them. I saw, too, something that radically altered my ministry: I could not truly love either that congregation or any other, nor could I love myself, until, I was emotionally independent, spiritually free.

It is a truth that applies not only to ministers but to people in all walks of life: *we can genuinely love, both others and ourselves, only when we are relatively free— free to be and become fully ourselves.*

I want to emphasize, though, that the freedom which is so basic to self-love can be obtained in most cases only at considerable cost.

A young person, for example, cannot fully appreciate his parents nor himself until he has paid the price of leaving home and putting some distance between himself and his family. Only when he has taken that frequently difficult step is he free to love both his parents and himself.

In a sense, however, that step must be taken again and again. Not only when we are in our late teens and early twenties but at many points in our lifetime we may have to break free before we can fully love. A woman, for instance, may have to break out of a destructive relationship, one in which it is impossible for her to love either her husband or herself. A man, again, may have to break away from a job which offers a comfortable future but little in terms of self-respect.

There are such times in life when we need to exchange security for the freedom that is essential to love. But the point is this: that exchange, however difficult it may be, proves almost invariably to be abundantly worthwhile.

* * *

Independence, without which love is impossible, can easily be, and often is, carried too far.

One day in a railroad station I offered to help an elderly woman with her luggage only to be curtly rebuffed. "No, thank you," she snapped, "I'm quite capable of carrying these bags myself."

In a sense that kind of sturdy independence is an admirable quality. It is good to see those who are pulling their own weight in a society that includes all too many lazy and irresponsbile people. In another sense, though, excessive independence is not a particularly attractive quality. In fact, it tends to alienate people, to turn them off, as I found that day in the station concourse.

I cannot, however, be too critical of that elderly traveler, for I have often been guilty of precisely the same thing. In my insistence on going it alone I have hurt people who wanted to help, especially when I was younger. Often, I remember, my parents offered to help me in one way or another and, just as often, in my silly independence and pride I said, "No, thank you." As I look back I appreciate immensely their patience and love, and at the same time I realize that if I had it to do all over again I would do it very differently. Given an opportunity to relive those years in which I was so determined to become my own person, I would, I think, be much more accepting of help and in that way contribute more to the interpersonal relationships that do so much to enrich our lives.

Basically, though, my history is typical. Over a period of decades, most of us, like myself, move through three stages. First there is the total and unavoidable dependence of infancy. Next, almost in reaction to that first stage, there is excessive and often rebellious independency, especially the independency of adolescence. Then finally the pendulum comes to rest somewhere in between the two extremes; we arrive at a position of interdependency, a more or less happy medium which is one of the distinguishing characteristics of a mature person.

According to Thomas Harris, author of *I'm OK—*

You're OK,[7] the bestselling and highly influential book on Transactional Analysis, there are four basic attitudes or positions which we take in relation to ourselves and others:

1. I'm not OK—You're OK
2. I'm not OK—You're not OK
3. I'm OK—You're not OK
4. I'm OK—You're OK

As preschoolers, says Harris, we find ourselves in the first position. We feel small, helpless, totally inadequate. In contrast we see our parents as great superior beings, almost as gods, omniscient and omnipotent creatures who can do no wrong. We say therefore, "I'm not OK—You're OK."

In some cases, Harris goes on to say, people skip with relative ease from the first to the fourth position. But in other cases—more specifically when they are deprived of "stroking" or love—people move from the first into the second or third position. Their resentment reaches out to include others as well as themselves. They say in effect, "I may not be much of a person, but I do feel that you've been most unkind" (I'm not OK—You're not OK). Or they say, usually as defiant adolescents, "I'm OK—I've made it this far—but the rest of you are just a bunch of outsized SOB's" (I'm OK—You're not OK).

Concludes Harris, maturity or mental health comes only when the person is able to affirm the worth of both others and himself: I'm OK—You're OK. To say that and mean it, says Harris, is to be truly Adult.

In Harris' scheme, too, we see something of the swing from extreme dependence all the way over to extreme independence and finally back again to a more central position, a combination of both extremes which is one of the distinguishing features of the truly mature person.

Certainly that happy combination of dependence and independence was characteristic of Jesus Christ. On the one hand he was the most sublimely independent person who ever lived. Everywhere in his society people bowed meekly before the civil and religious authorities. Everywhere they did as tradition demanded. Like sheep, they had no mind of their own; they simply yielded to the prevailing social pressures. But that was never true of Jesus. Always he was his own person—or, rather, his Father's person. Always he was obedient only to the voice of the Eternal, beyond and within. Again and again his family and friends urged him to play it safe, to yield a little, bend a little, compromise a little. Had he done so, he would no doubt have enjoyed wealth, popularity, and power and lived to a ripe old age. But no more uncompromising person ever lived.

On the other hand, though, this extraordinarily independent person never hesitated to appeal for assistance. As we read through the Gospels, we can see one instance after another in which he said to people, "I need your help," or words to that effect. To Simon the fisherman he said, right at the outset of his ministry, "I need your boat. Row me a few feet out into the lake, if you will, and let me preach from there to the crowds on shore."[8] To a Samaritan woman with a history of several marriages, licit and illicit, he said, "I need a drink of water."[9] To Mary and Martha, whose home was in the village of Bethany, and probably to a number of others he said, "I need food and a bed."[10] To an unknown man on the first Palm Sunday, he said through his disciples, "I need your donkey to carry me into Jerusalem."[11] To John Mark's mother he said, "I need a room in which my disciples and I can dine tonight."[12] It was their last meal together. Less than twenty-four hours later, the master's body was laid to rest—typically, in a borrowed tomb.[13]

It has been suggested that Jesus' frequent appeals for help were nothing more nor less than shrewd strategy on the part of an expert in human relations. After all, what better way to win friends and influence people than to admit to a certain helplessness and need? For my part, though, I believe that when Jesus appealed for help, as he so frequently did, he was acting in a perfectly spontaneous and natural way. He was not manipulating people. He was just being himself. But what a winsome self it must have been!

I believe, too, that in that life we see the ideal—not total dependence and not total independence but, rather, a superb combination of both.

*   *   *

Earlier the point was made that we must be free to be ourselves before we can fully love both ourselves and others.

But when we speak of being ourselves, we raise a fundamental question: *which* self? For the truth is that each of us consists of several selves.

"I am large," cried Walt Whitman, "I contain multitudes."[14] Well, so do we all.

As Thomas Kelly put it, "Each of us tends to be, not a single self, but a whole committee of selves. There is the civic self, the parental self, the financial self, the religious self, the society self, the professional self, the literary self. And each of our selves is in turn a rank individualist, not cooperative but shouting out his vote loudly for himself when the voting time comes."[15]

Or in the words of Robert De Ropp: "Sincere observation soon brings the student face to face with this fact. There is no single self. A man is one self at home and another at the office; one self at work, another when on vacation; one self with his wife, another with his secretary. Now and then, after some lapse of behavior, he may express astonishment or regret: 'I don't know what possessed me. That is not the real me, I forgot myself.' To which the careful investigator will reply, 'Forgot which self?' For it should be fairly obvious from the above that *multiplicity of selves is the common condition*. Existence of a single 'I' corresponding to a single aim and a single will is the exception rather than the rule."[16]

The point is that when, in our desire to be ourselves and be free to love, we set out to express ourselves we can choose for expression any one of a number of selves. We can be this, that, or the other self; we can, in fact, be any one of dozens of selves. So the question is: which self will it be?

Unfortunately, some counselors have suggested to their clients that the answer to that question lies in irresponsible self-expression. Most unwisely, these counselors have encouraged people to go out and let the libidinous self run wild. "Loosen up," they have urged. "Let yourself go. Don't allow yourself to be hampered by a lot of silly, old-fashioned scruples. Forget all that nonsense. 'If it feels good, do it!' Give free rein to your instincts, your passions, your whims, and that way you'll find the fulfilment you're seeking."

A growing number of counselors go even further by suggesting (presumably, only to their more attractive clients) sexual relations ("sex therapy") with the counselor himself. Great sport for the counselor! But all too often it serves only to compound the client's anguish.

Clearly what these counselors fail to recognize is that when we give full unbridled expression to our more primitive selves, when we give *irresponsible* vent to greed, laziness, anger, lust, and the like (all of which are part and parcel of our humanity and which, as such, deserve expression—provided, of course, that it is some kind of responsible expression) we do not contribute to self-love; we detract from it. We end up liking ourselves—and others too—not more but less.

On the other hand, when we consistently give expression to our finest selves we cultivate and confirm those selves; we become genuinely better people, more loving people, and, as such, people who have a higher opinion of themselves and, correspondingly, a deeper appreciation of others.

3.

ACCEPTING OURSELVES:

The Second Step in Loving Ourselves

Abraham Lincoln once stood in the slave market in New Orleans and watched black men and women being bought and sold like so many cattle. Shaken by the spectacle, an angry, glowering Lincoln muttered, "This thing is wrong, and if ever I get the chance, I'm going to hit it and hit it hard!"

John Howard, William Wilberforce, Elizabeth Fry, William Booth, and Florence Nightingale were others who were far from being accepting people, completely satisfied with the status quo. On the contrary, these men and women, and others like them, were fighters, out-and-out rebels, people haunted by a "divine discontent" who spent their wealth, energy, and time, their very lives, in the struggle for radical changes in the social order.

In our time too there are all kinds of evils that could be eliminated, at least in part. Poverty, disease, illiteracy, war, environmental pollution, the population explosion, and the galloping consumption of earth's non-renewable resources—clearly our duty is not simply to *accept* these evils. It is up to us to *overcome* them insofar as we can and make this confused and broken world a better place.

Also in our own lives there are some things that should be changed. Obesity, ignorance, alcoholic tendencies, undisciplined behavior—to accept these things, to shrug one's shoulders and say resignedly. "I'm afraid there's nothing much I can do about these problems but just go on living with them," is in most cases a great mistake.

But just as there are some things in our lives that should be changed so there are some things that should be accepted.

I like the story of the man who wrote the Department of Agriculture about the dandelions on his lawn. "Dear Sirs," he lamented, "My lawn is infested with dandelions. I have pulled them and sprayed them. I have used every device known to man. But still the dandelions keep multiplying. I am at my wits' end. Can you help me?" In due time he received a reply: "Dear Sir: Since you cannot get rid of your dandelions, we suggest that you learn to love them."

In everyone's life there are equivalents to those dandelions; there are misfortunes and limitations that cannot be eliminated and must therefore be accepted and integrated into the landscape of our lives. A physical handicap, a subnormal intelligence, a mediocre talent, an unfortunate marriage, or an unfulfilling job from which now there can be no responsible escape— these are only some of the situations that may seem cruelly unfair but that, nevertheless, have to be accepted with as much grace as possible.

In all this, of course, the last thing I want to suggest is that our limitations should be *prematurely* accepted. I believe that in some situations our best bet is to work with might and main to rise above a particular misfortune. But I believe, too, that often there comes a time when further effort is obviously futile and when, just as obviously, the best thing we can do is simply accept the inescapable and thereby, in some strange way, both dignify and enrich our lives.

"O Lord," goes the prayer often used by Alcoholics Anonymous, "give me the courage to change the things that can be changed, patience to accept the things I cannot change, and wisdom to know the difference." It is a good prayer, pointing as it does to the limitations that are inherent in everyone's life and that can be transcended only to the extent that they are accepted.

Basically it comes down to this: to accept one's limitations is to accept oneself *totally*. Like most people, I have no difficulty in accepting myself fractionally. Which is to say, I can accept my assets very easily and even gratefully, but not my liabilities. The point is, though, that only when I accept the less-than-good in myself along with the good can I accept myself *fully*.

It is also a fact that when we fail at this point, when our self-acceptance is merely fractional, we tend in our pursuit of excellence to overextend ourselves and, in so doing, become objects of ridicule or even worse.

A case in point is the older person who, instead of

accepting his wrinkles and bifocals, his thinning hair and thickening waist, resists the business of aging for all he is worth and who, in the process, becomes a caricature, perhaps even a grotesque caricature, of the young people he so desperately longs to emulate.

It was of just such people that Marya Mannes was obviously thinking when she wrote: "There is no trick in being young: it happens to you. But all this is obscured daily, hourly, by the selling barrage of youth, perhaps the greatest campaign for the arrested development of the human being ever waged anywhere. *Look young, be young, stay young,* they call from every page and on every airwave. You must be young to be loved. And with this mandate, this threat, this pressure, millions of goods are sold and millions of hours are spent in pursuit of a youth which no longer exists and which cannot be recaptured. The result of this is in woman, obscene; in man—pathetic."[1]

In many cases, too, the person who fails to accept himself becomes embittered and morose.

Here, for example, is Byron, born with a clubfoot. One of Byron's great contemporaries, Sir Walter Scott, was also a cripple. But while Scott simply accepted his misfortune, seldom giving it a second thought, Byron loathed his disability, brooded over it and became in the end a sour, cynical, disgruntled person.

Again and again we see similar misfortunes affecting people in entirely different ways, all of which serves to show that in many instances the critical or determining

51

factor in life is not what happens to us but how we respond to it. Provided we *accept* our lives, our limitations, our very selves, we can overcome almost anything.

When, however, we fail in this vital business of self-acceptance we do ourselves nothing but harm; in fact, we may even destroy ourselves.

It has sometimes been suggested that the colossal problems Napoleon caused for the people of a whole continent are due to the fact that he was such a *little* Corsican. If Napoleon had been a strapping six-footer, it has been speculated, he would not have been such a driven person, so possessed by an overweening desire to compensate for his smallness of stature by lording it over the whole of Europe. Possibly so.

Napoleon, however, was not unique. For in our time too there are any number of people who, instead of accepting their limitations and settling for a modest but perfectly comfortable existence, cause themselves no end of suffering by struggling relentlessly to achieve some kind of preeminence. I have relatives and friends like that, people whose ulcers and coronaries, neuroses, breakdowns, yes, and even deaths, stem basically from their stubborn insistence on achieving heights for which they were never equipped.

Kierkegaard has a beautiful parable in which he points to the devastating results of non-self-acceptance:

> There was once a lily that stood quite apart, near a little running brook, and was well acquainted with some nettles as well as a few other small flowers there in the neighbor-

hood. The lily was, according to the Gospel's veracious description, more beautifully arrayed than Solomon in all his glory, beside being carefree and happy the whole day long. . . .

But it happened one day that a little bird came and visited the lily; it came again the next day, and then it remained away for several days before it came again; which impressed the lily as being strange and inexplicable, inexplicable that the bird should not stay in the same place, like the small flowers—strange that the bird could be so capricious. But as so often happens, so too it happened to the lily, that because the bird was so capricious, the lily fell more and more in love with it.

The little bird was a bad bird; instead of putting itself in the place of the lily, instead of rejoicing with it in its beauty and innocent happiness, the bird wished to make itself important by feeling its own freedom, and by making the lily feel its bondage. And not only this, the little bird was also talkative, and it would tell all kinds of stories, true and false, about how there were, in other places, very unusually magnificent lilies in great abundance; how there were joy and gaiety, fragrance, brilliant coloring, a song of birds, which far surpassed all description. . . .

So the lily became troubled; the more it listened to the bird the more troubled it became. . . . Now it began to occupy itself with itself and with the circumstances of its life in its self-concern—so long was the day. . . . Said the lily, "My wish is not an unreasonable desire; I do not ask the impossible, to become what I am not, a bird, for example; my desire is only to become a splendid lily, or even the most splendid one." . . .

At last it confided absolutely in the bird. One evening they agreed that the next morning a change should take place which would put an end to the concern. Early the next morning came the little bird; with its beak it cut the soil away from the lily's roots, so that it might thus become free. When this was accomplished, the bird took the lily under its wing and flew away. The intention was, of course, that the bird would take the lily to where the magnificent lilies bloomed; then the bird would again assist in getting it planted down there, to see if, through the change of soil and the new environment, the lily might not succeed in becoming a magnificent lily in company with the many, or possibly even an imperial lily, envied by all the others.

Alas, on the way the lily withered. If the discontented lily had been satisfied to be lily, then it would not have become concerned; if it had not become concerned, then it would have remained standing where it was—where it stood in all its beauty; had it remained standing, then it would have been precisely the lily about which the preacher spoke on Sunday, when he repeated the Gospel's words: "Consider the lily. . . . I say unto you that even Solomon in all his glory was not arrayed like it." . . .

And if a man, like the lily, is satisfied with the fact of being human, then he does not become ill from temporal concern; and if he does not become temporally concerned, then he continues to stand in the place appointed to him; and if he remains there, then it is truly so, that through being human he is more glorious than the glory of Solomon."[2]

Kierkegaard's point was strikingly made: self-acceptance is essential to the full realization of our humanity.

But necessary though self-acceptance is, it is by no means easy. For many of us, in fact, it is so difficult that we resort to all kinds of useless substitutes: we ignore, belittle, and punish ourselves; we devote every energy to improving ourselves. But all the time the one thing we will not do, in so many cases, is simply accept ourselves.

Self-acceptance is especially difficult for young

people. In our teens and twenties we tend to be so upwardly mobile, so bent on getting ahead, that we do not particularly appreciate ourselves as we are. We want to be *more* than we are. By the time we get into our thirties and forties, we manage, some of us, to achieve a fair measure of contentment. But in most cases it is not until we are well along in years that our lives are characterized by the serenity of self-acceptance.

Self-acceptance can take, literally, a lifetime to learn. Even a lifetime is not enough for some people; death finds them still profoundly unhappy with themselves.

Speaking of this very difficulty, the difficulty of self-acceptance, Arthur Miller said through one of his characters: "I had the same dream each night—that I had a child; and even in the dream I saw that the child was my life; and it was an idiot. And I wept, and a hundred times I ran away, but each time I came back it had the same dreadful face. Until I thought, if I could kiss it, whatever in it was my own, perhaps I could rest. And I bent to its broken face, and it was horrible . . . but I kissed it. . . . I think one must finally take one's life in one's arms, Quentin."[3]

If we are wise we will do just that. Sooner or later we will say to ourselves, "I'm not all that I'd like to be, not by a long shot. Nevertheless I do have certain gifts that merit acceptance and even gratitude. That being the case, I intend to stop bewailing my inadequacies and limitations and, instead, accept myself, enjoy myself, and let the Almighty make out of me whatever he will."

It is worth reminding ourselves, too, that we have no

right to look to others for love and acceptance if we will not love ourselves. I may look to someone for love—for acceptance, appreciation, affection, and all the rest of it. But, if at the same time I refuse to love myself, I am asking that someone to do something I will not do myself, which is patently unfair.

Or to put it in more positive terms, we can legitimately look to others for love only when we love ourselves.

"My son," said one of the sages of long ago, "in all modesty, keep your self-respect and value yourself at your true worth. Who will speak up for a man who is his own enemy, or respect one who disparages himself?"[4]

Fundamental, however, to the whole business of self-acceptance is the acceptance not of some imaginary self but of one's *real* self.

Quite early in life we arrive at certain conclusions about ourselves, conclusions that are a result of the input we receive from the "significant others" in our lives: our parents, sisters and brothers, playmates, teachers, co-workers and friends. From all these people each of us gets the clear impression that he is a particular kind of person.

On the one hand, given enough approval, we may come to see ourselves as capable, attractive people with glowing prospects. On the other hand, subjected to year after year of relentless criticism, we may wind up with an extremely negative view of ourselves.

Too, the picture we have of ourselves may be either highly realistic or just the opposite, dismally inaccurate.

In those cases, though, where the self-image is both positive and realistic, the individual is off and running. Knowing that he has certain strengths, and having accepted those strengths along with his weaknesses, just as others have accepted him, he is free to turn his attention outward, to go out into the world, find ways of capitalizing on his gifts and build for himself a satisfying future.

In those other cases where the self-image is grossly unrealistic, where people think too highly or too poorly of themselves, the results are always the same: either they expect too much of themselves and life and thereby meet with nothing but frustration and disappointment or they settle for far too little.

Socrates urged, "Know thyself!" Wise counsel! For the fact is that we cannot accept what we do not know, including ourselves.

To repeat, it is not always easy to arrive at an understanding of ourselves. But easy or not, it is imperative. In the words of Harry and Bonaro Overstreet, "Not until the estimate (of oneself) is brought more or less in line with reality can the individual begin to feel at home with life and to fulfill his own capacities."[5]

*   *   *

A cartoonist showed a bearded, sandaled, and blue-jeaned artist saying to a sedate middle-aged visitor to the artist's avant-garde studio, "I paint what I like, and, by God, if I may say so, I like what I paint."[6]

It would be wonderful if all of us were so self-approving, for there is no doubt that if we were we would be happy indeed.

In his Sermon on the Mount, Jesus spoke of the happiness of the merciful, the meek, the peacemakers . . . [7] I wonder if there is not another beatitude that, just possibly, Jesus might have consented to add to the list: "Happy the person who accepts himself." It is easy to find examples of people for whom self-acceptance has obviously been the key to a new contentment.

In their best-selling book on the kind of behavior which they have termed "Type A" and which, in their judgment, is highly conducive to heart disease, Doctors Meyer Friedman and Ray Rosenman reported: "Recently, having observed an extraordinarily charming and relaxed doctor, one of us asked him how he avoided Type A behavior. He smiled and said, 'A few years ago, I faced up to the truth that I always had been and always will be a second-rate physican. After I realized this, it was quite easy to begin to relax.' "[8] Well, there is a man for whom self-acceptance has obviously been a liberating exercise, a source of serenity and delight.

We see the beginning of that kind of joy in the life of one of the characters in John Steinbeck's *Sweet Thursday*.[9] Fauna operates a brothel, but, unlike most madams, Fauna sees her girls as actual persons. She knows some are good for nothing but peddling their bodies. Others, though, are capable of becoming much more, and Suzy is one of this latter group. Aiming at Suzy's reclamation, Fauna sets up a date for the little tart with one of the town's leading citizens. Comes the big day and Suzy, whose experience with high-minded people has been absolutely minimal, is more than a little apprehensive. Before setting out on her big date, she says to Fauna a little nervously, "Is there anything I can do for you, Fauna?" Fauna's reply: "Yes, I want you should repeat after me, 'I'm Suzy and nobody else.' " Puzzled but cooperative the girl repeats, "I'm Suzy and nobody else." Fauna adds, "I'm a good thing." Now into the spirit of the exercise Suzy echoes, "I'm a good thing." Fauna then invites her to say, "There ain't nothing like me in the whole world." Suzy begins, "There ain't nothing . . ." But then she breaks down and cries. For the first time in her life she is beginning to appreciate her own worth, to accept her potential, and along with that appreciation there are tears, tears of joy.

What that passage suggests, too, is that self-acceptance is a prelude to growth.

Some of us have the idea that self-acceptance is inimical to personal growth. "As I see it," said a man who without meaning to was presenting quite a familiar point of view, "when we accept ourselves, we stop trying; we settle down and just stagnate."

The fact is, though, that when we truly accept ourselves, far from sinking into some kind of vegetative state we experience a real liberation of our latent powers, we become new persons, more relaxed, more productive, and more fulfilled.

How can that be? What happens is that when we accept ourselves we stop worrying about ourselves. Having accepted ourselves we can forget about ourselves and be free of ourselves; we can turn our interests and energies—which are no longer sapped by anxiety—*outward*, away from ourselves, and so deal with life in a vastly more creative way.

Harry and Bonaro Overstreet made this point when they said: "A genuine self-acceptance . . . makes the individual feel, with a new serenity, 'Well . . . I am at least what I am. I may not set the world on fire. But I can be myself and see what comes of it.' Such an attitude may seem to mean only that the individual is lowering his sights; unhitching his wagon from a star; accepting mediocrity as his lot. Yet this is not what happens. The valuable effect of the changed attitude is that it releases the individual from his consuming anxiety about himself and lets him do the one thing prerequisite to any realistic dealing with life: namely, *turn his attention outward*. It is this shift in the direction of attention that makes the patient say what he has not said before—and say it more thoughtfully."[10]

We find too that not only is self-acceptance characteristic of those who have begun the long climb to personal maturity but also it is characteristic of those who have "arrived"—insofar, that is, as any of us ever do arrive—those who are secure, confident, creative people.

"Self-actualizing people," Abraham Maslow termed them, and he described them beautifully when he said:

> They can accept their own human nature in the stoic style, with all its shortcomings, with all its discrepancies from the ideal image without feeling real concern. It would convey the wrong impression to say that they are self-

satisfied. What we must say rather is that they can take the frailties and sins, weaknesses, and evils of human nature in the same unquestioning spirit with which one accepts the characteristics of nature. One does not complain about water because it is wet, or about rocks because they are hard, or about trees because they are green. As the child looks out upon the world with wide, uncritical, innocent eyes, simply noting and observing what is the case, without either arguing the matter or demanding that it be otherwise, so does the self-actualizing person look upon human nature in himself and in others.[11]

*　　*　　*

A fact that needs to be emphasized is this: self-acceptance is contingent on the acceptance of others; we can accept ourselves only to the extent that we are accepted by a person or persons other than ourselves.

In some cases, I might add, the accepting person is not human but suprahuman—a Person.

It was this Person who so profoundly changed the lives of Saul of Tarsus, Augustine, Martin Luther, and John Wesley. All these people and scores of others underwent, literally, a hell of a time until quite suddenly there came sweeping over them a sense of the most ineffable acceptance. For the first time in their lives these grim and desperate individuals felt totally accepted and infinitely loved, not so much by their fellowmen as by God, and, as a result of that acceptance, they experienced an acceptance of self—an inner security and an extraordinary liberation of their powers—that enabled them to go out and change the world.

In our time too people are sometimes overcome by a feeling of acceptance that is absolutely ecstatic and that comes not from other people but directly out of the heart of the cosmos. It is at these times that, if only for a few moments, all the barriers come down. No longer does the person feel alienated, apart from the world. Instead he feels a tremendous sense of unity with the whole of creation, including the world of people. It is the unity of love. Everything and everyone, the individual and his neighbors as well, seem fused into one pulsing incandescent world of pure love. For some it is a religious experience of transcendent proportions. For others it is not perceived in religious terms. But for all who undergo this experience, there is a sense of *love* that is literally indescribable—the love of creation, the love of others, the love of God and, along with all this, the love of self. No one who has undergone this experience can help but feel in its wake a sense of self-worth that, without being in the least tainted by pride, is nothing short of sublime.

Perhaps, though, because ours is such a secular age, an age so largely devoid of religious experience, most of us rarely, if ever, experience the acceptance of God. This means, of course, that if we are to find the acceptance from beyond which is so necessary to the acceptance of self, we must find it in other people. Paul Tillich, who spoke so meaningfully to our secular society, put it in a nutshell when he said, "No self-acceptance is possible if one is not accepted in a person-to-person relationship."[12] Which is it exactly. Only insofar as we are accepted by others can we accept ourselves.

The small daughter of my good friends wrote an essay one day for her teacher. Entitled simply "Myself," the essay reads: "In 1967 a very nice girl was born on Remembrance Day. I will be 8 years old in November. In our family there are 10 people ... I was born at Grace Hospital. My father is a doctor. I help my mom by cleaning up my room. My favorite sport is tennis. At school I like to paint pictures. My special friends are Valary (*sic*), Karen, Susan, Nancy, and Dawn. When I have free time after school I like to play with Valary. When I grow up I want to by (*sic*) a nurse."

In that essay we see a self-love which is absolutely delightful: "In 1967 a very nice girl was born on Remembrance Day." How is such love to be explained? It is simple: richly loved by others—her parents, her brothers and sisters, her friends, Valerie, Karen, Susan, Nancy, Dawn, and all the rest of them—that little girl richly loves herself.

In the last analysis it is as simple as this: the more we are loved by others the more we tend to love ourselves.

It follows that if we are deficient in self-love, if we have an abysmally low opinion of ourselves and are most unhappy with ourselves, what we deeply need is to get into the company of some warm, comfortable, accepting people so that, accepted by them, we may be able to accept ourselves.

Perhaps in the past we have had far too much of

challenge and demand; people—our parents especially—almost from our infancy, have asked too much of us and have taught us to ask too much of ourselves. The result? Having failed to meet the expectations of all concerned, we have experienced a great deal of displeasure and rejection, both from without and from within. Clearly what we now need is a quite different group of associates. We need day in and day out to bask in the company of some kind, tolerant, easygoing people who will accept and appreciate us just as we are.

It should be stressed here that it is not enough to be accepted by those whose acceptance is essentially meaningless.

A girl, raised in a good home, left that home and set out on a way of life that represented a total rejection of many of the values she had been taught as a child. Drugs, heavy drinking, promiscuous sex, drifting from place to place, and general irresponsibility—all these became part and parcel of her new life-style. Predictably the results were far from good. In every way—mentally, physically, morally, and spiritually—she went downhill until eventually she was scarcely recognizable as the person she had been. One thing though had not changed: her need for acceptance. In fact, with her opinion of herself at rock bottom, she needed more than ever to be convinced of her acceptability. But where she erred at that point was in turning to the wrong people for acceptance—the dropouts and drifters, the derelict and disturbed, the failures, the losers, and the lost. It was only natural that she should turn to these people, for they were her friends. But somehow their acceptance was not enough. Repeatedly they said to her, "You're OK; you really are." But she remained unconvinced. Gradually, though, with little or no conscious planning she began to pull out of her slump. She started so improving every-thing about herself—her appearance and speech, her manners and morals—that she felt free to look for accep-tance to those who stood for something, those whose acceptance really counted. At last, knowing that she was accepted by these people, she was able to accept herself.

In our quest for self-acceptance we may have to do much the same thing; we may have to make ourselves acceptable, in our own eyes at least, to those whose acceptance we value, so that, having no doubts about our acceptability to others, we can accept ourselves.

As in the case of the girl I just mentioned, this may involve a general overhaul—an improvement of the total self with special emphasis perhaps on the moral self. Or it may involve reconciliation: going to the people from whom we have alienated ourselves, people whose accep-tance we prize, apologizing to them for our wrongdoing and, if necessary, making some kind of restitution.

Granted, it is not easy to meet such stringent condi-tions. But the fact is that there is no easy way to newness of life, especially for the morally delinquent and those who have made a mess of valued relationships. For them above all "the way is hard, that leads to life."[13]

It is precisely at this point that Protestantism so often fails. In the early days of its existence the Christian church required its members to confess their sins *publicly* and then to make the necessary reparations or undertake some appropriate penance. Gradually, however, the church lessened its demands. Confession, it said, need not be made publicly; confession need be made only to a priest. As for penance, in many cases all that was required of the wrongdoer was a mere token effort. Obviously life had become much easier for the transgressor. Then along came the Reformation and made it easier still. Said Protestantism: "Away with sacrament of confession. From now on, let Christian people confess their sins not to the clergy but directly to God, person-to-Person. Let Christians realize, too, that they do not have to struggle furiously in order to obtain salvation, for their salvation has already been paid for by the blood of Christ. All Christians have to do, therefore, is simply accept that salvation."

It was in this way that many of the clergy became guilty of dispensing, as Dietrich Bonhoeffer put it, "cheap grace."

In time, however, it became apparent that the "grace" was just as ineffective as it was cheap. People were assured that God loved them in spite of their sins but somehow they just could not believe it. No matter how often they were told that they were perfectly acceptable just as they were they did not *feel* acceptable. On the contrary, they felt guilt-ridden and even damned.

Psychiatrists too have failed the people they serve by dispensing cheap grace. Because there is no such thing as sin, some of them have said (we suffer from complexes, deviate tendencies, and neurotic and psychotic disorders but no longer from *sin*), and because our "aberrations" are not basically the fault of the individual (blame heredity, blame the environment, but don't, whatever you do, blame the individual) *there is nothing to atone for*. Simple! All the disturbed individual has to do, really, is relive his past in the presence of a completely nonjudgmental and accepting person, a professional whose whole approach is "value-free," and the patient will be relieved of his distress.

But again the trouble has been that in all too many cases the system just has not worked. People have undergone years of psychoanalysis at a cost of thousands upon thousands of dollars without feeling one bit better about themselves.

O. Hobart Mowrer, a past president of the American Psychological Association, stated the case in simple, trenchant terms when he said:

> We have tried to believe that personality disorder is basically an *illness—mental* illness; but we are now increasingly persuaded that the problem is fundamentally *moral*, that the guilt which is so obviously central in psychopathology is *real* rather than false, and that only a moral attack upon this problem can be successful. We had hoped that an easy solution might be found for personal evil; and we have tried both the doctrine of "cheap grace" (in religion) and the strategy of denying the reality of sin and guilt altogether (in psychoanalysis), but neither has worked. And so today there is a growing readiness to accept the verdict that

"therapy," or "salvation," is possible only at great cost: the cost of self-revelation, deep contrition, and a radically changed way of life.[14]

Mowrer has also speculated that much of the treatment we administer to the mentally ill may be healing because in their view *the treatment is a means of atonement*:

> So can it be that, lacking formal (institutional) recognition of the need for atonement following sin, modern men and women commonly make use, unconsciously, of the stigma, *dis*grace, and suffering connected with being "crazy" and hospitalized? Dr. Boisen has referred to the insane as the *self-condemned*; and to this we might add that they are also the *self-punished*. Depression is manifestly a form of self-inflicted suffering; and it has often been suspected that the reason why electroconvulsive shock "treatment" may speed the recovery of depressed persons is that it aids the work of expiation."[15]

We do not know, of course, to what extent that is true. But we do know that in many instances people hospitalized for mental illness have been put to work, say, polishing brasswork or scrubbing floors, have unconsciously perceived their toil as a form of penance, and have promptly recovered.

The point is, then, that for a number of people self-acceptance is a quality they once enjoyed, then lost, and must now recover. But for such people that recovery is not easy nor cheap. In fact it can be effected only at considerable cost, with the cost measured not in monetary terms but in terms of effort and pride.

Or to put it another way, in many (but by no means all) cases, self-acceptance is contingent on self-improvement. It is only as we improve ourselves—our behavior and dress, our manners and speech, our way of relating to other people—that we *feel* (not necessarily *are*) more acceptable to our neighbors and, so feeling, become more acceptable to ourselves.

4.

DISCIPLINING OURSELVES:

The Third Step in Loving Ourselves

Self-discipline, so fundamental to self-love, is by no means one of our society's more notable characteristics. In fact, the emphasis today, an emphasis to which we are all subjected, is on precisely the opposite of self-discipline, namely, self-indulgence.

"Don't be hampered by an old-fashioned morality," we are told, "by codes and commandments that should have been scrapped long ago. Loosen up, let yourself go! All those appetites and urges with which you were born—go along with them, give them free rein. As a people, we are too uptight and controlled. What we need is more spontaneity, more abandon. We need to go out and obey our impulses, gratify our desires, indulge our passions and whims. What we need, in short, is a far more freewheeling, fun-filled life."

As a reaction to the harsh restrictions of an earlier morality that point of view is eminently understandable. But the trouble is that those who advance that argument are not just reacting; they are *over*reacting, and in the process they are forgetting that, carried too far, liberty becomes license and license can be downright ruinous.

A distinguished educator, Dean Robert E. Fitch of the Pacific School of Religion, made the point when he said, "Young people today are losing control of their lives: having babies when they don't want them, getting married before they really want to, taking jobs before they are prepared for them. And this is 'the new freedom'!" Dean Fitch went on to point out that freedom is precisely what is being lost—"the freedom really to *choose* to get married, to *choose* to have a baby, to *choose* to take a job."[1]

Again and again people are being persuaded to abandon a self-disciplined way of life and, so persuaded, are ending up, in some cases, in a lamentable state.

I think, for example, of the shy, sensitive young woman who was advised by a perhaps well-intentioned but thoroughly misguided psychotherapist: "What you need, my dear, is to junk some of your old-fashioned scruples. Go out and live a little. Get involved with some lusty male. I think you'll find that if you relax some of your mid-Victorian standards, you'll be a much healthier and happier individual."

In helping the young woman to see that she needed to become a more open and outgoing person, the psychotherapist was unquestionably right. But where he was dead wrong was in pushing his case too far, in suggesting to his client that the way for her to achieve self-liberation was to go out and scrap her principles.

As it turned out, the woman did just that and ended up a full-blown psychotic—so tortured by guilt, so alienated from the world she had known before and from her finest self that escape into the twisted, eerie world of the schizophrenic seemed the only solution.

All of that, though, need never have happened if only the psychotherapist had recognized that *one of our fundamental needs is to submit to something higher than ourselves.*

Alfred Adler maintained that, above all else and to compensate for the total dependency and frequent humiliation we experienced as small children, we crave some kind of superiority. We want to be in a position where we, not others, are giving the orders.

Granted there is a wealth of truth in Adler's contention. But there is another side to the coin, namely that, along with our desire for self-determination, there is also our desire to submit.

Basically we are creatures who incorporate all kinds of opposing tendencies: good and evil, introvert and extravert, male and female (*yang* and *yin*), dominant and submissive. We talk sometimes about all the polarities in the outside world but all the time we ourselves are full of them.

As for our submissive tendencies, they probably date back to our primitive beginnings when man's very survival depended on belonging to a group which functioned under some kind of authority. Without that strong central authority the group would have perished. Recognizing this, man submitted, and has been submitting ever since.

Put simply, it pays to submit. When we place ourselves under the authority of some powerful person or group we obtain some distinct benefits: we enjoy a certain prestige, one which the "small independent operator" never knows; we enjoy too a relief from the necessity of having to plot our own course (a process which can involve a lot of difficult decisions); and, per- haps most important of all, we enjoy a deep sense of security or belonging.

A Dietrich Bonhoeffer may speak of mankind's "coming of age." But the fact is that, both individually and collectively, there is still something of the child in all of us, something that actually hungers for authority and for the benefits that life under authority confers.

It is to this hunger that a man like Adolf Hitler appeals when he says in effect, "Submit to my authority, and I will lead you into a golden age—an age of unparalleled prosperity and prestige."

Always there are people who respond to that kind of appeal. But when they do, when they say goodbye to their better judgment and blindly give themselves into the hands of some charismatic demagogue, they display submissiveness carried too far, carried so far, in fact, that it becomes downright suicidal.

In excess, then, submissiveness can be masochistic. Here, for example, is a girl who, for some deep, perverted reason, needs to be humiliated and hurt and who, accordingly, goes out and gets involved with a sadistic partner, a man who takes genuine delight in in- flicting pain—black eyes, broken bones, and all the rest of it. At first people are inclined to be sympathetic. "What a girl!" they say. "How amazingly loyal! Anyone else would have left that animal long ago." But gradually the tune changes, until in the end people are criticizing her for being such a doormat. "It's pathetic," they say of her martyrdom. "No, it isn't pathetic, it's just plain sick," as indeed it is.

In moderation, however, there is nothing wrong with submissiveness. As a matter of fact it is perfectly normal, part and parcel of our very being, as evidenced, for example, by our hero-worshipping tendencies. Deep down we all long for someone (or Someone) to idolize and emulate. For the small child, as often as not, this someone is his father or mother. Later on, it can be someone quite different—a rock singer, a sports celebrity, a movie star. We are amused by these crushes of youth, or irritated by them! But all too often we forget that we adults have precisely the same need, the need to pay obeisance to something or someone beyond ourselves.

In fact, to deny this need is to deprive ourselves of life's deepest meaning. Everywhere today there are people who demand "absolute freedom" (as if there were any such thing)—freedom from custom, from conventional morality, from obligations to family and community, and from just about everything else that smacks of responsibility and restraint. Of all people, though, these are in the end the most miserable. Why? Because they forget that life without love, loyalty, devotion, and worship is scarcely worth living.

Harry Emerson Fosdick expressed this truth in an impressive way when he said:

> Man is made for self-surrender—Toscanini to Beethoven, the mother to her babe, the lover to the loved, friend to friend, the scientist to his research, the social servant to his cause, the saint to his Master. Throughout life at its best this basic impulse to self-submission runs, as ennobling when well used as it is debasing when it is perverted. All superior achievement has this motive in it—whether it be John Masefield, a mill hand in Yonkers, reading Keats for the first time and overcome by the conviction that his life belonged to poetry, or Jesus in the Garden, praying, 'not my will, but thine, be done'—and neither a good citizen in daily life nor a martyr dying for his cause is conceivable without it.[2]

What it amounts to, really, is that submission is inescapable. Because of what we are, because of our essential nature with its built-in appetite for both dominance and submission, we simply *must* submit ourselves to something, if not to the highest and the best, then inevitably to mediocrity or worse: to the tyranny of public opinion perhaps, to charlatans and demagogues, to alcoholism or lust, to boredom and futility, meaninglessness and despair; in fact to all kinds of ugliness and evil.

The sages and saints point also to a strange paradox: in submitting ourselves to some transcendent greatness, we experience not servitude or bondage but, rather, a freedom that is sheer joy. The Bible and the Koran, the Upanishads and the Buddhist scriptures, the Tao-te-

Ching, the teachings of Confucius and the works of Plato, Spinoza, Descartes, and Kant all make the same point: it is in bondage to the Sublime that true freedom is found.

The Book of Common Prayer speaks of God as One "whose service is perfect freedom." It may seem strange to find those two words "service" and "freedom" in such close juxtaposition. But certainly that is where they belong, for the service of greatness does indeed go hand in hand with human freedom.

George Matheson expressed this truth in a familiar hymn:

> Make me a captive, Lord,
> And then I shall be free;
> Force me to render up my sword,
> And I shall conqueror be.
> I sink in life's alarms
> When by myself I stand;
> Imprison me within Thine arms,
> And strong shall be my hand.
>
> My heart is weak and poor
> Until it master find;
> It has no spring of action sure—
> It varies with the wind.
> It cannot freely move,
> Till Thou hast wrought its chain;
> Enslave it with Thy matchless love,
> And deathless it shall reign.

*   *   *

One of man's most basic needs is to grow. Philosophers all the way from Aristotle to Bergson and beyond, and some of the greatest figures in the world of psychology—Carl Jung, Kurt Goldstein, Karen Horney, Otto Rank, Erich Fromm, Carl Rogers, and Rollo May, to name only a few—are unanimous in saying that one of man's most distinctive characteristics is his urge to improve himself.

Perhaps no one has made the point so convincingly as the late Abraham Maslow. Deep within all of us, said Maslow, is "the desire to become more and more what one is, to become everything that one is capable of becoming."[3] In a later work he wrote: "It looks as if there were a single ultimate value for mankind, a far goal toward which all men strive. This is called variously by different authors, self-actualization, self-realization, integration, psychological health, individuation, autonomy, creativity, productivity, but they all agree that this amounts to realizing the potentialities of the person, that is to say, becoming fully human, everything that the person can become." [4]

But now the question: how do we realize our human potential? How do we become all that we are capable of becoming?

Part of the answer to that question is that growth is to some extent a perfectly natural process. A small child, for instance, does not have to make a conscious effort to grow. In his or her case, growth—far from being planned, scheduled, forced, contrived—is completely spontaneous, something that just *happens*. In later life, too, growth—though perhaps not physical

77

growth—is largely a gift. We do not have to work for it, struggle for it, pay for it. We simply accept it. Without the least planning or effort on our part, we become, in one way or another, improved people.

But there is more to it than that, for growth is also a product of self-discipline.

Especially in later life, beyond that point at which we tend to "peak" (physically, in our mid-twenties or thereabouts; intellectually, artistically, and otherwise, considerably later), the only way we can even maintain our level, much less improve it, is to deal with ourselves in quite a disciplined way.

Certainly too the only way largely to realize our human potential is through rigorous self-discipline.

Sometimes we look half-enviously at the person who has achieved great heights and say to ourselves, "It was easy for him. Most of us have to struggle for whatever little eminence we manage to achieve. But, because he has been blessed with all kinds of natural ability, he has been an automatic success."

In all probability, that admired person is indeed immensely gifted. But the chances are, too, that another key factor in his superiority is unrelenting effort. For years, perhaps even decades, he toiled like the proverbial Trojan to get to the top.

Pablo Casals, probably the greatest cellist of all time, used to spend hours on a single phrase, days and weeks on a single movement. As a matter of fact, he spent whole years on the Bach *Suites for Unaccompanied*

Violoncello. Commented Casals: "People say I play as easily as a bird sings. If they only knew how much effort their bird has put into his song."

Not only in the realm of the arts but in other realms too—in business and government, in science and sports, in fact in every realm of human endeavor, including the realm of the spirit—greatness is generally achieved only at great cost.

But just as it is true that those who discipline themselves tend to grow and develop, so also it is true, conversely, that those who fail to discipline themselves tend gradually to deteriorate.

Life it seems has a built-in downward bias, which is partly what theologians mean when they talk about original sin. Just as a garden left untended will gradually be overrun by weeds and just as a piece of iron left exposed to the elements will gradually fall prey to rust so human nature if it is not deliberately cultivated will gradually go downhill.

Self-discipline, then, is not an option; it is a *must*—a must, that is, if we are to avoid that degenerative process.

It is also a fact that self-discipline is essential to self-esteem.

I am thinking now of a particular man, a gifted professional. A few years ago, in every way—physically, mentally, morally, and spiritually—he was keeping himself under good control and was right at the top of the heap, a successful and happy person. Gradually, however, he relaxed his grip. One discipline after another went by the boards. His dissolution went further and further until finally he was quite a different person. On the face of it he was doing well enough. But those who knew him could see the great gaping cracks behind the smooth façade; they could see a man who was functioning at only a fraction of his former efficiency and who, at the same time, was a gloomy, despondent person, lower in terms of self-respect than he had ever been in his life.

It can be argued, I know, that in his case the despondency came first and the general laxity afterward, that the despondency was, in fact, the cause of the laxity. It is more likely, though, that in that instance the reverse was true: it was the failure in self-discipline that led to such a loss of morale.

On the other hand, there are those who deal with themselves in quite a disciplined way, even though that may not be obvious, and who at the same time are unusually secure and productive people—individuals whose lives attest to the fact that again and again self-discipline and self-love go hand in hand.

* * *

A Canadian government television plug for physical fitness recently made the point that the average 30-year-old Canadian male is in about the same physical condition as his 60-year-old Swedish counterpart. Presumably that criticism applies not only to Canadians but to Americans too. Here we are, we North Americans, among the most affluent people on earth, but by no means notable for our physical condition. We eat too much, many of us, with our diet consisting largely of a wide assortment of junk foods. We smoke and drink to excess and certainly we do not exercise enough. Rather than walk we will take an elevator up a single floor or drive a mere couple of blocks to mail a letter. It is no wonder that we are overweight, short of breath, and all too prone to a variety of illnesses and an early grave. When we permit that kind of physical deterioration we do nothing to contribute to a high opinion of ourselves and of life in general.

Chances are, we all know the greatly overweight person who is all smiles and chuckles but who, beneath that smiling exterior, carries more than his share of hostility. There are the somber eyes which belie the smiling face, and there is the frequency with which, ever so subtly, he digs at other people—the little barbs, the veiled allusions. All these point to someone whose fundamental unhappiness with everything and everyone is essentially a projection of his dissatisfaction with his own person.

We can see the same thing, a lack of self-appreciation, not only in some overweight people but also in the alcoholic, the chain smoker, the compulsive worker, the battered old pug with the cauliflower ear and the badly scrambled brains who keeps hoping for another shot at the title; we can see it, in fact, in almost anyone who subjects his or her body to gross abuse.

It goes almost without saying that when people like

that deal with themselves in a more disciplined way they do a great deal to add to their self-respect. Self-discipline—tough, physical self-discipline—is often conducive to self-esteem.

It is significant that social workers are now having a good deal of success in rehabilitating delinquent teen-agers, many of them from the slums of our large cities, by taking them out into wilderness areas—on long canoe trips, for example—and subjecting them to a really punishing existence. For days and even weeks on end the young people have to cope with heat, cold, drenching rain, mosquitoes, a Spartan diet, head winds, high waves, and long back-breaking portages. But as often as not they emerge from these ordeals with a bright new appreciation of themselves and their abilities.

In the interest of self-respect, it is important too that we discipline ourselves mentally.

Like our other capacities, our mental capacities need occasional exercise: they need to function sometimes at full capacity; they need to be stretched and extended. Without that, in fact, they tend to lose something of their potency.

I once talked with a southern Alberta farmer who told me that his land was irrigated from subterranean streams. In those streams, he said, there were tiny fish which were sometimes pumped up along with the water and which were totally blind. After generations of life in those deep lightless waters, the species' optic nerves had completely atrophied, leaving the fish without even a vestige of sight.

Our powers of mind, unlike the fishes' powers of sight, are never totally lost because there is always at least *something* to occupy them and keep them busy. But the point is that a mere something is not enough. What our minds need at every stage in our lives is some vigorous exercise. Only that can maintain our mental efficiency.

I remember visiting a delightful old lady, then in her nineties. Much to my surprise I found her engrossed in a best-selling and highly controversial book. It was a book which was by no means easy reading and which presented a point of view absolutely antithetical to some of the Christian fundamentals she had accepted as a child, a book that could easily have undermined her whole faith. But there she was, grappling with the issues it raised. Amazed, I asked, "Don't you find that an upsetting book?" "Yes, I do," she admitted. "But there's this about it: it makes me *think*, and that's good for me." She had the right idea. It is good for us deliberately to wrestle with deep issues and difficult problems. It helps to keep our minds elastic and keen.

We have the idea, some of us, that as we grow older our minds inevitably lose their sharpness, their edge. But that is not necessarily true. Experts have now established that, *given enough stimulation*, our minds can grow and develop until we are fifty, sixty, seventy, and even beyond.

In the realm of morality, too, self-discipline is fundamental to self-love.

When we lead morally responsible lives, seeing to it

that our passions and appetites are expressed in socially acceptable ways, we tend to be accepted and loved, not only by others but also by ourselves.

On the other hand, when we fall into serious misbehavior we become unacceptable both to others and to ourselves; we dislike and even despise ourselves.

According to some psychologists, a good deal of the mental illness in our society is basically a result of bad behavior. An individual does something wrong, and as a result feels so unacceptable to all concerned, so *guilty*, that he falls prey, perhaps to a mild neurosis, perhaps even to a full-fledged psychosis.

In these cases, according to the psychologists, the only way for the person to overcome his illness is to deal with himself in quite a stern and rigorous way: admit to his wrongdoing, rectify his behavior, and make whatever amends he can. Only when he has done that, they say, will he feel forgiven, accepted and loved, by other persons and by himself.

One of the nation's foremost psychologists, O. Hobart Mowrer, made precisely this point when he said:

> If one takes the neurotic's guilt seriously, that is, if (as now seems likely) 'neurosis' is just a medical euphemism for a 'state of sin' and social alienation, therapy must obviously go beyond mere 'counseling,' to self-disclosure, not just to a therapist or counselor, but to the 'significant others' in one's life, and *then* on to active redemption in the sense of the patient's making every effort within his power to undo the evil for which he has previously been responsible.[5]

Still another area in which self-discipline can contribute immensely to self-love is the spiritual realm.

For centuries past, the church has urged its members to make faithful use of "the means of grace"—Holy Communion, public worship, Bible study, and prayer. Engage systematically in these exercises, the church has said, and the chances are excellent that you will become a better person—inwardly stronger, more sensitive and kind, and, not least of all, happier with yourself.

A great many people today are seeking spiritual growth in just such conventional ways. Every Sunday finds them in church or synagogue, and every weekday studying the Scriptures and saying their prayers.

A great many others, though, are involved in an amazing variety of (more or less) spiritual exercises that are anything but conventionally Christian—Zen, Hindu, Sufi, humanistic, mechanical (biofeedback, for example), eclectic, and occult.

It has been estimated that one of those ways, Transcendental Meditation, now claims over half a million followers in America alone. Every day, for some twenty minutes before breakfast and another twenty minutes before dinner, these people, representing all age groups and all walks of life, settle themselves into a comfortable position and, using certain techniques, invite a profoundly restorative sense of peace. These are disciplined people, and it is their very discipline, self-imposed, that contributes so much to their spiritual health and self-appreciation.

* * *

Carried too far, almost any virtue becomes a vice. We all know, for example, the man who prides himself on his forthrightness. "As far as I'm concerned," he says, "there's no beating around the bush. I speak my mind. Granted I'm not the most tactful person in the world, and granted too I sometimes get people a little upset. But there's this about me: I'm honest, I tell it like it is."

There is no doubt that there is much to be said for candor. But there is no doubt either that when candor is carried too far, when it is expressed at the expense of kindness, it ceases to be a virtue and becomes a vice.

So too with a number of the other virtues: in heaping amounts they can easily be more demonic than divine.

In excess, for instance, thrift becomes miserliness, industriousness becomes an exercise in masochism, and patriotism becomes "the last refuge of scoundrels." In excess too optimism becomes blind to life's sterner realities; kindness edges into sugar-coated sentimentality, devoid of any backbone and bite, and hard-headed realism loses its ability to laugh and sing, becoming a gray, mechanical way of looking at life, utterly lacking in poetry and passion.

Self-discipline too can be overdone and can, in that event, be inimical to personal and interpersonal development.

More specifically, self-discipline is wrong when it results in pride.

I think, for example, of the man who spends hours each week in suntanning, lifting weights, and in general cultivating the body beautiful. He is, without a doubt, a superb physical specimen—all rippling, bulging muscles and glowing good health. But there is something else he has acquired along the way: a swelled head of substantial proportions. In his case, unfortunately, physical fitness has found a partner in pride.

I think, too, of the man who is busy cultivating not his body but his soul. He studies his Bible, says his prayers at great length both morning and night, and sees to it that his morals are above reproach. But the upshot of it all is that he is no saint; he is a twentieth-century Pharisee, all puffed up with self-righteousness and described by one of his acquaintances as "an absolute pain in the neck." Better for him if he were to ease up on the self-discipline and be a little more human!

We are in error too when we see self-discipline as a means to self-improvement, with that self-improvement viewed as essential to the approval of others (or even God).

In some cases, as we have noted, self-improvement is necessary and right. When, for example, a person is obese, alcoholic, or intelligent but illiterate, he would be foolish *not* to dig into an appropriate self-improvement program. In fact, if he does not do that, he stands every chance of being unacceptable both to others and to himself.

In other cases, though, self-improvement is not really necessary. It is unnecessary because the person is *already* acceptable to others. His wife and children and his friends and business associates all find him more than adequate as a human being. Unfortunately, however, the man himself has great difficulty in believing that. In Tillichian terms, he just cannot accept the fact of his own acceptability. He does not *feel* acceptable to others and, because of that, he does not feel acceptable to himself either. What to do? Well, as he sees it, there is only one thing to do: so improve himself that he will be acceptable to all concerned. With this in mind, he drives himself almost into the ground in a desperate, unrelenting effort to become a better person. But all so needlessly! If only he would see that he is OK just as he is!

In some cases, then, self-improvement is essentially neurotic in that it is born out of deep personal insecurity and an altogether false perception of oneself and one's situation.

Ideally, self-improvement does not precede self-acceptance; it follows it. Ideally, self-improvement is not a means to acceptance (by others and by the self) but an *expression* of self-acceptance. We feel good about ourselves and happy with life in general, and, because we feel that way, quite spontaneously we plunge zestfully into, say, a three-credit course in the English literature of the seventeenth century.

Well, there is the ideal: self-improvement for its own sake; self-improvement for the sheer fun of it; self-development pursued in one way or another not because the person *needs* to but because he *wants* to. In the last analysis once again it is all a matter of balance.

Self-discipline is fine provided it does not so outweigh self-being that the person becomes in effect a mechanical man—rigid, controlled, and largely devoid of freedom, spontaneity, and a sense of fun.

Similarly, self-discipline is fine provided it does not overrule self-acceptance—as it did for a long time, for instance, in the lives of St. Paul, Martin Luther, and John Wesley, people who went through spiritual torment until eventually they came to understand that self-discipline without self-acceptance is a dead end street leading only to frustration and despair.

So the point is this: *when self-being, self-acceptance, and self-discipline are properly combined in a person's life, then that person in all probability will be a self-loving individual and, as such, a whole, happy, and effective human being.*

5.

HELPING OTHERS TO LOVE THEMSELVES:

A Postscript

We can help people, you and I, in all kinds of ways. We can feed them, clothe them, and shelter them. We can arrange to have them educated in one or more of thousands of subjects. We can see to it that they are provided with money, recreation, medical treatment, and any number of other essentials and amenities. But most of all, perhaps, we can help people by helping them to love themselves. Our husbands and wives, our children and the other children in our lives, our friends, neighbors, and business associates—possibly the most important thing we can do for these people is contribute to their self-appreciation.

How do we go about helping people to love themselves? The answer is simple: we love them.

But this raises a further question: *How* precisely do we go about loving other people? It is all very well to say that it is necessary for us to love those others so that they in turn may be able to love themselves. But what does that mean? What exactly is entailed in the love that invites self-love?

The answer to that question is suggested in the previous chapters of this book. There we saw that the person who loves himself is one who *is* himself, who *accepts* himself, and who *disciplines* himself. But what we now see is that these three functions—self-being, self-acceptance, and self-discipline—emerge as a response to the way a person is treated. *When, over the years, other people allow a person to be himself, accept him as he is, and at the same time help him to live within certain limits, he tends to appropriate these attitudes; he learns to be, accept, and discipline himself.*

It is up to us, then, in our dealings with others, to accord them the freedom to be themselves, giving them that freedom not grudgingly but in a spirit of genuine acceptance, and to balance that kind of acceptance with a suitable amount of challenge or demand. For it is in so doing that we demonstrate the kind of love that calls forth self-love.

There is no doubt though that all too often we fail to strike that balance. Again and again in our relationships with other people, we *demand*, yes, but we do not *accept*. Instead of gladly allowing those other people to express their God-given individuality, we try to mold them into quite different persons.

Especially at home we are prone to apply great pressure to the people to whom we are closest, with the object of the exercise being to refashion their lives into a style that to us seems more acceptable.

I think, for example, of the scholar who married a girl who is by no means his intellectual equal. His wife has beauty, charm, and great artistic gifts. But instead of gratefully accepting his wife's considerable assets and at the same time overlooking her odd liability, the man is toiling away, trying to bring his wife up to his own Ph.D. level and make her a more "cultured" person.

Similarly a number of wives are bound and determined that they are going to get their husbands to lose weight, to stop smoking, to be more sociable, and to improve their manners, their morals, their skills, their status, and just about everything else. In scores of ways, some subtle and some thunderingly obvious, a great many husbands are under pressure from their wives to improve themselves and their performance.

We see the same unfortunate tendency in the way many parents deal with their children. These are the parents who, far from being content with what their children are, want their children to be different, better, and who, accordingly, are making an all-out effort to refashion their children's lives.

I once knew an ex-Olympic athlete (we will call him Bill and say that he had been a hurdler) who had a son (named, significantly, Bill *Junior*) and whose efforts to make another world-class hurdler out of his son were nothing short of cruel. I do not think I have ever known a more bullied and brow-beaten child, nor one so seething with suppressed resentment.

Similarly there are a great many of us who are trying diligently to turn our children either into little replicas of ourselves, which is impossible, or into creatures totally alien to their talents and interests: athletes, musicians, scholars, "Christians," and all the rest of it.

What we fail to recognize is that when, in our non-acceptance of another person, we set out to fashion him into someone other than he is, we say to him by implication, "I don't love you as you are," and when we say *that* to people we make it extremely difficult for them to love themselves.

Granted there are some cases in which people *should* be changed or helped to change. Criminals should be rehabilitated, illiterate people educated, and sick people healed. In fact, many of the institutions in our society—schools, hospitals, churches, and social agencies—are dedicated to effecting just such changes.

However, even though there are some people who need help in changing the nature and direction of their lives, what the great majority of people need is simple acceptance and, along with that acceptance, the freedom to be themselves—freedom from the pressure to be other than they are, freedom to move along lines that, for them, are natural and right.

What I am pleading for is *tolerance* in our dealings with one another, the tolerance that is one of love's most distinguishing characteristics and that, as such, is supremely conducive to self-love.

Examples of this kind of tolerance? There are all kinds of them.

Benjamin Disraeli, a case in point, was one of the brightest luminaries of his time—a man with foppish tendencies, yes; a man of vaulting ambition and something of a schemer, again yes; but, for all that, a man of towering ability. Eventually Disraeli married a woman who, unlike her highly polished husband, was lamentably lacking in the social graces. She was overweight and her taste in clothing was ofttimes bizarre. In her dealings with people she was often insensitive, tactless, and rude. In many ways she was everything that her husband was not. But Disraeli, the most accepting of husbands, loved his wife, loved her dearly, loved her just as she was.

I saw something of the same superb tolerance in my own home. My mother was a refined, fastidious, and cultured person, a woman who came out of a blue-collar background but who was a born aristocrat. Slim and attractive, she had a high intelligence and a passion for the arts, for good books, and for great music. Ballet, opera, and symphony were for her a sheer delight. My father, on the other hand, was easily identified with his origins. Raised on a farm he remained in many ways a farm boy all his life. Eventually he became a distinguished clergymen, a warm-hearted, outgoing man with literally thousands of friends. But he was no sophisticate. He tended to shop for clothes in bargain basements, to go to symphony concerts and fall sound asleep, and to sneeze and blow his nose with an explosive vigor that must have startled some people almost to the point of cardiac arrest! I am sure that my mother was dismayed by some of the things he did and said. But she never indicated that and she never tried to change him. Even though he differed from her in a hundred ways, she loved him just as he was and respected him immensely. It was a happy marriage, one of the happiest I have ever seen.

I have known parents who dealt with their children in the same marvelously accepting way. I think, for instance, of the Harvard professor who did not raise even the slightest objection when his eldest son set out to major in motor mechanics. "Go to it," he said. "I don't think everyone needs a university degree." I think too of the prominent minister, another Ph.D., who helped his son get established in the gravel-hauling business. People questioned the man's wisdom. But as the minister himself put it, "Well, if that's what Bob wants, that's fine with me."

What it comes down to is this: when we adopt that attitude, when we accord other people, especially the members of our family, the freedom to be themselves, and when we do so in a generous spirit, we demonstrate a respect for their individuality, their essential personhood, their right to choose and to be, that contributes incalculably to their respect for themselves.

Another thing we do for people when we free them to be themselves is this: we invite their growth and development; we invite a fuller realization of their human potential.

A number of people have the idea that the way to make other people productive is to *pressure* them. With that in mind and in their dealings with other people— their employees, for instance, or their children—they are forever prodding, pushing, and cracking the whip. "The more pressure I apply," they reason, "the more I'll get in terms of results."

What these people fail to understand is that pressure can be counterproductive. When we bear down heavily on people, demanding of them nothing less than top performance and total productivity, all that happens in a great many cases is that we get them so tied up in knots that they simply cannot function.

On the other hand, though, and this is a strange paradox, when we relieve people of the pressure to be and to do what we want, when we say to them, "I want you to do it your way," we give them wings: we set them free and make it possible for them to achieve heights that otherwise would be quite unattainable.

Often young people are pressured by ambitious parents to become statesmen, artists, scientists, attorneys, and so on. But, having no aptitude for these professions, the students fail miserably. At that point, in many cases, the parents wash their hands of their offspring and give them free rein to go ahead and do whatever they please. The result? These "misfits" and "failures" set out in unexpected directions and blossom like the proverbial rose.

We need to recognize that, while we help people to love themselves by accepting them, we also help them by presenting them with a certain amount of challenge.

Basically what we have to do is strike a balance between these two attitudes of acceptance and demand.

This balance is essential in raising a family. We have to accept our children, but we have to discipline them too.

Sometimes our children object that we are too hard on them, as perhaps we are. But the fact is that children appreciate a certain amount of discipline, provided, of course, that it is an expression of genuine goodwill.

A sociologist once questioned a group of teenagers on their feelings about their parents. He was surprised to learn that the boys and girls who had been brought up permissively were not at all enthusiastic about the whole experience. At the same time, those who had been wisely disciplined were clearly grateful for the kind of upbringing they had received.

One girl in particular told the interviewer that she lived in an apartment building in a big city. After supper in the summertime, she said, the children in the block used to gather out in the street for play. But gradually the group would dwindle away. One girl would say that she had to go home because her mother had told her to be in before eight o'clock. A father would whistle and a boy would head for home. Or a mother would call and a whole family of children would leave the group. "They would all go," said the girl. "It would get dark and I would be there alone, waiting for my father or my mother to call me in. They never did."

It is true, of course, that children do not always appreciate discipline at the time they are being subjected to it. But often in later life they express appreciation of parents who cared enough to impose a few limits.

Studies have shown that parents who strike that happy balance between acceptance and demand are most likely to have children who rate high in terms of self-esteem.

A few years ago Dr. Stanley Coopersmith and his associates looked closely into the lives of eighty-five "preadolescents of middle class background who were male, white, and normal."[1] After concluding the study, Coopersmith reported: "All our results indicate that the parents of children with high self-esteem are significantly *less* permissive than are the parents of children with less self-esteem."[2] The psychologist went on to say: "The most general statement about the antecedents of self-esteem can be given in terms of three conditions: total or nearly total *acceptance* of the children by their parents, clearly defined and enforced *limits*, and the *respect* and latitude for individual action that exist within the defined limits. In effect, we can conclude that the parents of children with high self-esteem are concerned and attentive toward their children, that they structure the worlds of their children along lines they believe to be proper and appropriate, and that they permit relatively great freedom within the structures they have established."[3]

We learn from that and other studies that, even though they may not always appreciate it, children do thrive on the right kind of discipline.

Adults too are most likely to become happy and productive people, loving both others and themselves, when life offers them a combination of acceptance and challenge.

I do not mean to suggest, of course, that at every stage in their lives people need a 50-50 mix—acceptance and challenge in equal proportions. Our needs vary, both from person to person and from time to time. One person may need total acceptance, while another may need a good stiff challenge. Again a particular person may need boundless acceptance at one stage in his life and at another stage a much more demanding relationship.

When to accept and when to challenge? It is not easy to answer that question. In answering it, indeed, we sometimes need all the wisdom we can muster, especially in view of the fact that to accept when we should be challenging, or vice versa, can be downright ruinous.

We need wisdom too in determining *how much* to challenge. We need that wisdom because when we challenge people too little we do not particularly help them while, on the other hand, when we challenge them too much we cause them to throw up their hands in despair and cry, "I give up, I'll never make it."

When, however, we are able to deal with people as their needs dictate, offering them now acceptance and now challenge, and, in general, a good mixture of both, we can be immensely helpful.

A few years ago life dealt me a jolting blow. Deeply hurt I confided one day in a little group of my colleagues, and their response turned out to be exactly what I needed. A couple of members of the group were sympathetic. "We're awfully sorry," they said. "We really feel for you," and I knew they did. No friends could have been more accepting and kind. The other member of the group, however—a man who can be both acutely perceptive and exceptionally blunt—took an entirely different tack. "Ray," he said, "this isn't like you. I've always thought a lot of you, and it bothers the hell out of me when I see you wallowing in self-pity." I was stung by his statement, but it did me good, and I see now how fortunate I was in having friends who together extended acceptance and challenge in a superb combination.

*   *   *

One thing more needs to be said: when by loving others, when by enabling them to be, accept, and discipline themselves, we help people to love themselves, and we invite their love, which in turn contributes to our self-love.

What we see here is the beginning of an upward spiral which is lost eventually in the love of God: by being, accepting, and disciplining ourselves we come to love ourselves; in loving ourselves we love others as well; in loving those others and expressing that love in a judicious combination of acceptance and demand we enable them to love themselves; loving themselves they

love us too; their love fuels our self-love; loving ourselves all the more we express that self-love in terms of
other-love; and so it goes, on and on, and up and up,
until ultimately, if not in time then in eternity, we
achieve that perfect Love which is the destiny of the
human soul.

NOTES

1. The All-importance of Loving Ourselves

1. Louis J. Bragman, quoted in June Callwood, *Love, Hate, Fear, Anger and the Other Lively Emotions* (Garden City, N.Y.: Doubleday & Co., 1964), p. 49.

2. Erich Fromm, quoted in Callwood, *Love, Hate, Fear.*

3. Michel E. de Montaigne, "Essais." Quoted in John W. Gardner, *Self-Renewal* (New York: Harper & Row, 1964), p. 111.

4. Grace Stuart, *Narcissus* (London: George Allen & Unwin, 1956), p. 138.

5. Luke 10:27.

6. Heinz L. and Rowena R. Ansbacher, eds., *The Individual Psychology of Alfred Adler* (New York: Basic Books, 1946), p. 358.

7. Harry Emerson Fosdick, *The Power to See It Through* (New York: Harper & Bros., 1935), p. 176.

8. Quoted in Robert Short, *The Parables of Peanuts* (New York: Harper & Row, 1968), p. 86.

9. Sigmund Freud, *Collected Papers*, vol. 4, translated under the supervision of J. Riviere (London: Hogarth Press and Institute of Psycho-Analysis, 1925), p. 46.

10. Stuart, *Narcissus,* p. 139.

11. Freud, *Collected Papers*, vol. 5, p. 81.

12. Raymond B. Blakney, trans., *Meister Eckhart* (New York: Harper & Bros. 1941), p. 204.

13. Søren Kierkegaard, *The Works of Love*, trans. D. F. and L. M. Swenson (Princeton, N.J.: Princeton University Press, 1946), p. 17.

2. Being Ourselves: The First Step in Loving Ourselves

1. Edith Sitwell, *English Eccentrics* (New York: Vanguard Press, 1957), p. 23.

2. Ibid., p. 88.

3. Ibid., p. 119.

4. Romans 12:2.

5. Martin Buber, *Hasidism and Modern Man,* ed. and trans. M. Friedman (New York: Horizon Press Publications, 1958), pp. 139-40.

6. William G. Cole, *The Restless Quest of Modern Man* (New York: Oxford University Press, 1966), p. 83.

7. Thomas A. Harris, M.D., *I'm OK—You're OK: A Practical Guide to Transactional Analysis* (New York: Harper & Row, 1967).

8. Luke 5:3.

9. John 4:7.

10. Luke 10:38-39.

11. Matthew 21:1-3; Mark 11:1-3; Luke 19:28-34.

12. Matthew 26:17-19; Mark 14:12-16; Luke 22:7-13.

13. Matthew 27:57-60; Mark 15:42-46; Luke 23:50-53; John 19:38-42.

14. Walt Whitman, "Song of Myself," in *Leaves of Grass* (Philadelphia: David McKay, 1900), p. 92.

15. Thomas R. Kelly, *A Testament of Devotion* (New York: Harper & Bros., 1941), p. 116.

16. Robert S. De Ropp, *The Master Game* (New York: Delacorte Press, 1968), p. 93.

3. Accepting Ourselves: The Second Step in Loving Ourselves

1. Marya Mannes, quoted in James L. Christensen, *Creative Ways to Worship* (Old Tappan, N.J.: Fleming H. Revell Co., 1974), p. 107.

2. Søren Kierkegaard, *The Gospel of Suffering*, trans. D. F. and L. M. Swenson (Minneapolis: Augsburg, 1948), pp. 178-83. Used by permission.

3. Arthur Miller, *After the Fall* (New York: Viking Press, 1964), p. 24.

4. Ecclesiastes 10:28-29.

5. Harry and Bonaro Overstreet, *The Mind Alive* (New York: W. W. Norton Co., 1954), p. 54.

6. David Langdon in *The New Yorker Album of Art and Artists* (Boston: New York Graphic Society Ltd., 1970).

7. Matthew 5:3-13.

8. Meyer Friedman and Ray H. Rosenman, *Type A Behavior and Your Heart* (New York: Fawcett World Library, 1974), p. 220.

9. John Steinbeck, *Sweet Thursday* (New York: Viking Press, 1954), p. 146.

10. Overstreet, *Mind Alive*, pp. 67-68.

11. Abraham H. Maslow, *Motivation and Personality* (New York: Harper & Bros., 1954), pp. 206-7.

12. Paul Tillich, *The Courage to Be* (London: Collins, Fontana Library, 1962), p. 161.

13. Matthew 7:14.

14. O. Hobart Mowrer, *The Crisis in Psychiatry and Religion* (New York: D. Van Nostrand Co., Insight Books, 1961), p. 190.

15. Ibid., p. 100.

4. Disciplining Ourselves: The Third Step in Loving Ourselves

1. Quoted by Norman Vincent Peale in *Reader's Digest*, November 1965, p. 268.

2. Harry Emerson Fosdick, *On Being a Real Person* (New York: Harper & Bros., 1943), p. 181.

3. Abraham H. Maslow, *Motivation and Personality* (New York: Harper & Bros., 1954), p. 92.

4. Abraham H. Maslow, quoted in Frank G. Goble, *The Third Force* (New York: Pocket Books, 1974), p. 92.

5. O. Hobart Mowrer, *The Crisis in Psychiatry and Religion* (New York: D. Van Nostrand Co., Insight Books, 1961), p. 108.

5. Helping Others to Love Themselves: A Postscript

1. Stanley Coopersmith, *The Antecedents of Self-Esteem* (San Francisco: W. H. Freeman & Co., 1967), p. 8.

2. Ibid., p. 183.

3. Ibid., p. 236.